TEACHER'S PET PUBLICATIONS

LITPLAN TEACHER PACK
for
The Contender
based on the book by
Robert Lipsyte

Written by
Mary B. Collins

© 1996 Teacher's Pet Publications
All Rights Reserved

This **LitPlan** for Robert Lipsyte's
The Contender
has been brought to you by Teacher's Pet Publications, Inc.

Copyright Teacher's Pet Publications 1996

Only the student materials in this unit plan (such as worksheets, study questions, and tests) may be reproduced multiple times for use in the purchaser's classroom.

For any additional copyright questions,
contact Teacher's Pet Publications.

www.tpet.com

TABLE OF CONTENTS - *The Contender*

Introduction	5
Unit Objectives	7
Reading Assignment Sheet	8
Unit Outline	9
Study Questions (Short Answer)	13
Quiz/Study Questions (Multiple Choice)	20
Pre-reading Vocabulary Worksheets	33
Lesson One (Introductory Lesson)	43
Nonfiction Assignment Sheet	45
Oral Reading Evaluation Form	47
Writing Assignment 1	49
Writing Assignment 2	60
Writing Assignment 3	65
Writing Evaluation Form	61
Vocabulary Review Activities	62
Extra Writing Assignments/Discussion ?s	54
Unit Review Activities	67
Unit Tests	71
Unit Resource Materials	105
Vocabulary Resource Materials	119

A FEW NOTES ABOUT THE AUTHOR
Robert Lipsyte

Robert Lipsyte was born on January 16, 1938 in New York City. He graduated from Columbia University in 1957 and almost immediately began his writing career with the *New York Times* as a copyboy and later a sports reporter. Mr. Lipsyte has also worked for the *New York Post*, CBS-TV as a sports essayist for *Sunday Morning*, NBC-TV as a sports correspondent, PBS-TV as host of the program *The Eleventh Hour*, and as a journalism teacher and radio commentator.

Mr. Lipsyte has written several books from an edited collection of his sports columns, to a biography of Muhammad Ali, to young adult fiction. Robert Lipsyte's works of fiction for young people are usually about young people who through work and ethical standards grow into responsible, productive citizens. They also usually portray a realistic view of sports in the lives of everyday people. In *The Contender* (1967), his first noteworthy young adult novel, Mr. Lipsyte drew on his experiences as a sports reporter and combined them with his philosophy about the role of sports in the everyday lives of everyday people.

Other novels Mr. Lipsyte has written include *One Fat Summer, Summer Rules, The Summerboy, Jack and* Jill, and *The Brave* (a sequel to *The Contender*).

INTRODUCTION - *The Contender*

This unit has been designed to develop students' reading, writing, thinking, and language skills through exercises and activities related to *The Contender* by Robert Lipsyte. It includes eighteen lessons, supported by extra resource materials.

The **introductory lesson** introduces students to one main theme of the novel through a bulletin board activity. Following the introductory activity, students are given a transition to explain how the activity relates to the book they are about to read. Following the transition, students are given the materials they will be using during the unit. At the end of the lesson, students begin the pre-reading work for the first reading assignment.

The **reading assignments** are approximately thirty pages each; some are a little shorter while others are a little longer. Students have approximately 15 minutes of pre-reading work to do prior to each reading assignment. This pre-reading work involves reviewing the study questions for the assignment and doing some vocabulary work for 8 to 10 vocabulary words they will encounter in their reading.

The **study guide questions** are fact-based questions; students can find the answers to these questions right in the text. These questions come in two formats: short answer required or multiple choice. The best use of these materials is probably to use the short answer version of the questions as study guides for students (since answers will be more complete), and to use the multiple choice version for occasional quizzes. It might be a good idea to make transparencies of your answer keys for the overhead projector.

The **vocabulary work** is intended to enrich students' vocabularies as well as to aid in the students' understanding of the book. Prior to each reading assignment, students will complete a two-part worksheet for approximately 8 to 10 vocabulary words in the upcoming reading assignment. Part I focuses on students' use of general knowledge and contextual clues by giving the sentence in which the word appears in the text. Students are then to write down what they think the words mean based on the words' usage. Part II nails down the definitions of the words by giving students dictionary definitions of the words and having students match the words to the correct definitions based on the words' contextual usage. Students should then have an understanding of the words when they meet them in the text.

After each reading assignment, students will go back and formulate answers for the study guide questions. Discussion of these questions serves as a **review** of the most important events and ideas presented in the reading assignments.

After students complete reading the work, there is a **vocabulary review** lesson which pulls together all of the fragmented vocabulary lists for the reading assignments and gives students a review of all of the words they have studied.

A lesson is devoted to the **extra discussion questions/writing assignments**. These questions focus on interpretation, critical analysis and personal response, employing a variety of thinking skills and adding to the students' understanding of the novel.

The **project** which follows the discussion questions has students working to create goals for themselves and plans by which they could achieve their goals.

There are three **writing assignments** in this unit, each with the purpose of informing, persuading, or having students express personal opinions. The first assignment is to express personal opinions: students tell whether or not they think they are "contenders." The second assignment is to inform: students state their goal(s) and the plans by which the goal(s) will be achieved. The third assignment is to persuade: students write the script for a scene between James and Alfred when Alfred tries to persuade James to become a contender.

In addition, there is a **nonfiction reading assignment**. Students are required to read a piece of nonfiction related in some way to *The Contender*. After reading their nonfiction pieces, students will fill out a worksheet on which they answer questions regarding facts, interpretation, criticism, and personal opinions. During one class period, students make **oral presentations** about the nonfiction pieces they have read. This not only exposes all students to a wealth of information, it also gives students the opportunity to practice **public speaking**.

The **review lesson** pulls together all of the aspects of the unit. The teacher is given four or five choices of activities or games to use which all serve the same basic function of reviewing all of the information presented in the unit.

The **unit test** comes in two formats: all multiple choice-matching-true/false or with a mixture of matching, short answer, multiple choice, and composition. As a convenience, two different tests for each format have been included.

There are additional **support materials** included with this unit. The **unit resource section** includes suggestions for an in-class library, crossword and word search puzzles related to the novel, and extra vocabulary worksheets. There is a list of **bulletin board ideas** which gives the teacher suggestions for bulletin boards to go along with this unit. In addition, there is a list of **extra class activities** the teacher could choose from to enhance the unit or as a substitution for an exercise the teacher might feel is inappropriate for his/her class. **Answer keys** are located directly after the **reproducible student materials** throughout the unit. The student materials may be reproduced for use in the teacher's classroom without infringement of copyrights. No other portion of this unit may be reproduced without the written consent of Teacher's Pet Publications, Inc.

UNIT OBJECTIVES - *The Contender*

1. Through reading Lipsyte's *The Contender*, students will consider the merits of being a "contender," of taking charge of one's own life, setting goals and achieving them.

2. Students will demonstrate their understanding of the text on four levels: factual, interpretive, critical and personal.

3. Students will set a goal and think through a plan for achieving that goal.

4. Students will be given the opportunity to practice reading aloud and silently to improve their skills in each area.

5. Students will answer questions to demonstrate their knowledge and understanding of the main events and characters in *The Contender* as they relate to the author's theme development.

6. Students will enrich their vocabularies and improve their understanding of the novel through the vocabulary lessons prepared for use in conjunction with the novel.

7. The writing assignments in this unit are geared to several purposes:
   a. To have students demonstrate their abilities to inform, to persuade, or to express their own personal ideas
      Note: Students will demonstrate ability to write effectively to <u>inform</u> by developing and organizing facts to convey information. Students will demonstrate the ability to write effectively to <u>persuade</u> by selecting and organizing relevant information, establishing an argumentative purpose, and by designing an appropriate strategy for an identified audience. Students will demonstrate the ability to write effectively to <u>express personal ideas</u> by selecting a form and its appropriate elements.
   b. To check the students' reading comprehension
   c. To make students think about the ideas presented by the novel
   d. To encourage logical thinking
   e. To provide an opportunity to practice good grammar and improve students' use of the English language.

8. Students will read aloud, report, and participate in large and small group discussions to improve their public speaking and personal interaction skills.

READING ASSIGNMENT SHEET - *The Contender*

Date Assigned	Chapters Assigned	Completion Date
	1-4	
	5-8	
	9-13	
	14-16	
	17-20	

UNIT OUTLINE - *The Contender*

1 Introduction	2 PVR 1-4	3 Study ?s 1-4 PVR 5-8	4 Study ?s 5-8 Writing Assignment 1	5 PVR 9-13
6 Study ?s 9-13 Grammar Worksheet	7 PVR 14-16	8 Study ?s 14-16 PVR 17-20	9 Study ?s 17-20 Extra ?s	10 Quotes
11 Project	12 Writing Assignment 2	13 Vocabulary	14 Library	15 Nonfiction Reports
16 Writing Assignment 3	17 Review	18 Test		

Key: P=Preview Study Questions V=Prereading Vocabulary Worksheet R=Read

STUDY GUIDE QUESTIONS

SHORT ANSWER STUDY GUIDE QUESTIONS - *The Contender*

Chapters 1-4
1. Who is Alfred Brooks?
2. How is Alfred different from the gang at the clubroom?
3. Why did Major, James, Hollis, and Sonny go to Epstein's?
4. Why did Major, Hollis, and Sonny beat up Alfred?
5. When Aunt Pearl asked Alfred what had happened to him, what did he reply? Why?
6. Why did Alfred first go to Donatelli's Gym?
7. What did Uncle Wilson always ask Alfred?
8. Before he went to bed Sunday night, Alfred thought, ". . . Slave. Nothing's promised you.

Chapters 5-8
1. Why did the policemen stop Alfred in the park?
2. How did Mr. Epstein show he did not trust Alfred on the Monday after the attempted robbery?
3. Describe the relationship between James and Alfred.
4. What kind of a man was Bud?
5. Why did Alfred go to Madison Square Garden?
6. Why did Mr. Donatelli stop Willie's fight?
7. Identify Spoon.
8. What did Major want Alfred to do?
9. Why did Alfred stand up to Major? What was the result?

Chapters 9-13
1. What announcement did Alfred make at breakfast to explain why he appeared to be"drunk"?
2. What advice did Mr. Epstein give Alfred about boxing?
3. Why did Alfred go to the clubroom?
4. When James and Alfred finally meet at the clubroom weeks after the robbery attempt, what do they say to each other?
5. Why did Alfred go riding with Major, Hollis and Sonny?
6. Where did Alfred go after running away from the police?
7. Where did Alfred go after work on Monday?
8. Why did Alfred return to training after "quitting"?
9. How did Mr. Epstein show his renewed confidence in Alfred?
10. How did Alfred "earn" his mouthpiece?

Chapters 14-16
1. Why did Charlene think Alfred was sick? What was he actually doing?
2. What had happened at the clubroom since Alfred was last there?
3. Spoon made an offer to Alfred. What was it?
4. When Jackson fell down and stayed down, what did Alfred think? Why?
5. Did Alfred win his first fight? What was Mr. Donatelli's reaction?
6. Aunt Pearl, concerned for Alfred, lightly complained about his boxing. He replied, "I don't know about nothing else." What was her reply to him, and what did she mean?
7. What did Alfred discover he had in common with his aunt?

The Contender Short Answer Study Guide Page 2

8. Why wasn't Alfred going to quit boxing after his first fight?
9. Why did Alfred feel sick after his second fight?
10. Mr. Epstein gave Alfred a day off. Why?
11. For what volunteer job did Lynn and Harold try to recruit Alfred?
12. What did Alfred do on his afternoon off?

Chapters 17-20
1. How did Uncle Wilson view Alfred's wins?
2. Alfred came to a decision which surprised Aunt Pearl. What was it?
3. Who was the shuddering old man who crouched alongside Alfred's stairs? What did he want?
4. What did Mr. Donatelli tell Alfred after his third fight? Why?
5. Why did Mr. Donatelli allow Alfred one more fight?
6. Why were the police looking for James?
7. What did Alfred do for James?

SHORT ANSWER STUDY GUIDE QUESTIONS - *The Contender*

Chapters 1-4

1. Who is Alfred Brooks?
   Alfred is a young, black man living in Harlem. He is the main character of the novel. He works at Epstein's store as a stock boy and janitor.

2. How is Alfred different from the gang at the clubroom?
   He works and goes to church and tries to stay out of trouble.

3. Why did Major, James, Hollis, and Sonny go to Epstein's?
   They wanted to rob the cash register.

4. Why did Major, Hollis, and Sonny beat up Alfred?
   Alfred forgot to tell them about the silent alarm, and because of that, they nearly got caught by the police.

5. When Aunt Pearl asked Alfred what had happened to him, what did he reply? Why?
   He told her a dog knocked him off of a stone wall. He knew she would worry about him if he told her the truth; he would rather lie and give her a little peace of mind.

6. Why did Alfred first go to Donatelli's Gym?
   He was tired of being afraid of stronger gang members, and he wanted to be somebody, a champion.

7. What did Uncle Wilson always ask Alfred?
   He asked, "Been thinking about your future?" or "Been thinking about the trades?".

8. Before he went to bed Sunday night, Alfred thought, ". . . Slave. Nothing's promised you. Slave. Opportunity for advancement? You have to start by wanting to be a contender." What did he decide?
   He decided to begin training, to be a contender.

Chapters 5-8

1. Why did the policemen stop Alfred in the park?
   He fit the profile of a suspicious person -- a young black man running in the park. They assumed he was running from something, not just for sport.

2. How did Mr. Epstein show he did not trust Alfred on the Monday after the attempted robbery?
   He asked him if he knew anything about the attempted robbery, and he had someone else make the bank deposits.

3. Describe the relationship between James and Alfred.
   They were best friends as kids. They were slowly growing apart as young adults. After James got caught for the robbery, they were very distant. Alfred missed his old friend, but he was not interested in participating in James' new lifestyle of crime and drugs.

4. What kind of a man was Bud?
   Bud knew his place as Mr. Donatelli's assistant. He was an older man, experienced, firm but fair, and possessed a sense of humor.

5. Why did Alfred go to Madison Square Garden?
   Mr. Donatelli had left tickets for him to go watch a fight.

6. Why did Mr. Donatelli stop Willie's fight?
   He stopped the fight ". . . to save him from being hurt and to save him . . . from showing himself a coward in front of the crowd."

7. Identify Spoon.
   Bill Witherspoon was a former fighter managed by Mr. Donatelli. He went on to become a teacher after his boxing career. He met Alfred at Willie's fight.

8. What did Major want Alfred to do?
   He wanted him to cut the alarm wires at Epstein's.

9. Why did Alfred stand up to Major? What was the result?
   He had things he wanted to do, and being involved with a crime would mess up his future, so he refused Major. Major backed down and gained a new respect for Alfred.

Chapters 9-13
1. What announcement did Alfred make at breakfast to explain why he appeared to be "drunk"?
   He announced his boxing career. His enthusiasm for his new direction gave him a happiness and enthusiasm, which his family members noticed.

2. What advice did Mr. Epstein give Alfred about boxing?
   He told Alfred to give it up. He said that it is hard work for nothing; one can't make a living at it because it is full of racketeers and crooked managers.

3. Why did Alfred go to the clubroom?
   He wanted to see James and he was frustrated with what he felt was a lack of progress in his boxing career.

4. When James and Alfred finally meet at the clubroom weeks after the robbery attempt, what do they say to each other?
>Alfred apologized for not warning him about the alarm. James accepted the apology. Later Alfred discovered that James was using drugs, and he tried to convince him to stop. James just snapped back at Alfred, and Alfred passed out.

5. Why did Alfred go riding with Major, Hollis and Sonny?
>He was feeling hung-over, the guys told him he needed a break from work, and it was easier to go than to refuse.

6. Where did Alfred go after running away from the police?
>He went by the beach to the movies. Then he just walked past the gym and on home.

7. Where did Alfred go after work on Monday?
>He went to the movies and then to clean out his locker at the gym.

8. Why did Alfred return to training after "quitting"?
>He didn't really want to quit in the first place; he was just frustrated and somewhat confused. His talk with Mr. Donatelli gave him enough hope to relieve his frustration. Also, his days without training were slow and pointless.

9. How did Mr. Epstein show his renewed confidence in Alfred?
>He told him he would show him how to work the register and do "some other things" at the store, giving him more responsibility.

10. How did Alfred "earn" his mouthpiece?
>He knocked down Jose in a sparring round.

Chapters 14-16

1. Why did Charlene think Alfred was sick? What was he actually doing?
>She thought he was sick because he stayed in bed late. He was actually resting up for his big first fight.

2. What had happened at the clubroom since Alfred was last there?
>It was raided by the police who had found marijuana and heroin there.

3. Spoon made an offer to Alfred. What was it?
>He said he and his wife would help Alfred find a night school when he would be ready to go back for his high school diploma.

4. When Jackson fell down and stayed down, what did Alfred think? Why?
>He thought Jackson just didn't want to get up. He didn't want to believe that Jackson was really hurt.

5. Did Alfred win his first fight? What was Mr. Donatelli's reaction?
>Yes, he won his first fight. Mr. Donatelli said that winning wasn't enough.

6. Aunt Pearl, concerned for Alfred, lightly complained about his boxing. He replied, "I don't know about nothing else." What was her reply to him, and what did she mean?
   She said, "Before the summer you didn't know about boxing neither." She meant that if he could learn boxing, he could learn other things.

7. What did Alfred discover he had in common with his aunt?
   She had a dream once, too. Unlike Alfred, though, she never had the chance to reach for her dream.

8. Why wasn't Alfred going to quit boxing after his first fight?
   He wants to know how good he can be.

9. Why did Alfred feel sick after his second fight?
   He knocked out Griffin. He didn't want to hurt him; the thought that he could have really hurt or killed him made him sick.

10. Mr. Epstein gave Alfred a day off. Why?
    Alfred's mind obviously wasn't on his work. Epstein noticed that and figured that Alfred needed some time for himself.

11. For what volunteer job did Lynn and Harold try to recruit Alfred?
    They wanted him for their new recreation program. "The kids would really look up to a boxer."

12. What did Alfred do on his afternoon off?
    He went to a movie.

Chapters 17-20
1. How did Uncle Wilson view Alfred's wins?
   "Top fighters can make contacts with big people, get opportunities."

2. Alfred came to a decision which surprised Aunt Pearl. What was it?
   He decided to go back to school and get his high school diploma.

3. Who was the shuddering old man who crouched alongside Alfred's stairs? What did he want?
   He was James. James wanted money to buy drugs.

4. What did Mr. Donatelli tell Alfred after his third fight? Why?
   He told him it was time to retire because he didn't have the killer instinct.

5. Why did Mr. Donatelli allow Alfred one more fight?
   He let Alfred go one more fight so Alfred would also know it was time for him to retire.

6. Why were the police looking for James?
   He had broken in to Epstein's store again.

7. What did Alfred do for James?
	He found him at their "cave" and saved his life by convincing him to go to a hospital. From their conversation, one can assume that Alfred will do all he can to help James have a more meaningful life.

MULTIPLE CHOICE STUDY GUIDE/QUIZ QUESTIONS - *The Contender*

Chapters 1-4

1. Which of the following statements does not describe Alfred Brooks?
    A. Alfred is a young, black man living in Harlem.
    B. He is a member of a close-knit family consisting of his parents, two sisters, one brother, and an aunt.
    C. He works at Epstein's store as a stock boy and janitor.
    D. He is a junior in high school.

2. How is Alfred different from the gang at the clubroom?
    A. He carries a knife instead of a gun.
    B. He is the only one who can read.
    C. He is the only one who wants to admit girls to the club.
    D. He works and goes to church and tries to stay out of trouble.

3. Why did Major, James, Hollis, and Sonny go to Epstein's?
    A. They wanted to get jobs.
    B. They wanted Alfred to give them free candy bars.
    C. They wanted to rob the cash register.
    D. They wanted to buy some snacks to keep at the clubroom.

4. What did Major, Hollis, and Sonny do to Alfred after their trip to Epstein's?
    A. They beat him up.
    B. They turned him upside down and shook all of the money out of his pockets.
    C. They kicked him out of the club.
    D. They congratulated him and told him what a great guy he was.

5. True or False: When Aunt Pearl asked Alfred what had happened to him, he told her a dog knocked him off a stone wall. He knew she would worry about him if he told her the truth.
    A. True
    B. False

6. Why did Alfred first go to Donatelli's Gym?
    A. He thought he might be able to get a better paying job there.
    B. He hoped to get free tickets to some fights.
    C. He did it on a dare from Henry.
    D. He was tired of being afraid of stronger gang members, and he wanted to be somebody, a champion.

7. What did Uncle Wilson always ask Alfred?
    A. He asked "Do you have a girlfriend yet?" and is she cute?"
    B. He asked, "Been thinking about your future?" or "Been thinking about the trades?"
    C. "Have those white people you work for given you a raise yet?"
    D. He asked, "Are you treating you Aunt Pearl and your cousins right?"

The Contender Multiple Choice Study/Quiz Questions Page 2

8. Before he went to bed Sunday night, Alfred thought, "...Slave. Nothing's promised you. Slave. Opportunity for advancement?   You have to start by wanting to ----." Which of the following phrases finishes the statement?
    A. "...get your education."
    B. "...get what you can from Man."
    C. "...be a contender/do your best."
    D. "...get out of bed in the morning and be glad you have a chance to start again."

The Contender Multiple Choice Study/Quiz Questions Page 3

<u>Chapters 5-8</u>

9. True or False: The policeman stopped Alfred in the park because they thought he was being chased by a gang and wanted to help him.
   A. True
   B. False

10. How did Mr. Epstein act toward Alfred on the Monday after the attempted robbery?
    A. He asked Alfred if he knew anything about the attempted robbery, and then had someone else make the bank deposits.
    B. He pretended nothing had happened.
    C. He was very hostile and suspicious. He grilled Alfred about his friends and his activities, and threatened to fire him.
    D. He tries to make Alfred feel guilty by reminding Alfred of all he (Mr. Epstein) had done for Alfred and the community in general. Then he made a big show of forgiving Alfred and still trusting him.

11. Describe the relationship between James and Alfred.
    A. They were second cousins and enjoyed each other's company.
    B. They had met within the last year and were just getting to know each other, although they got along right away.
    C. They didn't really like each other, but they hung out together because they had mutual friends.
    D. They were best friends as kids. They were slowly growing apart as young adults.

12. Which of the following statements does not describe Bud?
    A. He was older and had a lot of experience.
    B. He was firm and fair.
    C. He was ambitious, and wanted to eventually take over the gym.
    D. He had a good sense of humor.

13. Where did Alfred go with Henry?
    A. He went to Greenwich Village to visit a friend of Henry's.
    B. He went to Madison Square Garden.
    C. He went to Radio city Music Hall.
    D. He went to Staten Island.

The Contender Multiple Choice Study/Quiz Questions Page 4

14. Why did Mr. Donatelli stop Willie's fight?
    A. He did it because he found out there was supposed to be a gang fight in the stands during the eighth round. He wanted to get his boys out before the trouble started.
    B. He did it because someone told him that Willie had been taking steroids.
    C. He did it because the other manager offered him a large sum of money to throw the fight. Donatelli needed the money to keep his gym open, so he agreed to stop the fight.
    D. He did it to save Willie from being hurt and to keep him from showing himself a coward in front of the crowd.

15. Who is Spoon?
    A. Bill Witherspoon was a former fighter managed by Donatelli. He went on to become a teacher after his boxing career.
    B. Tom Spoonson was Donatelli's first manager, who encouraged Donatelli to keep up the sport.
    C. Sam "the Spoon" Corey was friend of Donatelli's from his earliest fighting days. They had trained together. Sam was famous for his "spoon punch", which he had invented. He went on to become a famous middle-weight, and then financed the gym for Donatelli.
    D. Jim Evans was a trainer who sometimes worked with Donatelli's most promising young contenders. He was called "Spoon" because of his ability to "dish out" compliments, confidence, and criticism whenever each was needed.

16. What did Major want Alfred to do?
    A. He wanted him to steal the money from the Epstein's cash register by himself to prove he was worthy of joining the gang.
    B. He wanted him to give the other gang members a schedule of the times the store was the least crowded.
    C. He wanted Alfred to cut the alarm wires at Epsteins.
    D. He wanted him to implicate the members of a rival gang in the recent robbery.

17. What was Alfred' response to Major's request?
    A. He did what Major wanted for two reasons: He was afraid of what Major and the others would do to him if he didn't, and he hoped that by doing what Major wanted he would win back James' friendship.
    B. He refused to do it because he had things he wanted to do. His goals did not include being involved in the gang

The Contender Multiple Choice Study/Quiz Questions Page 5

Chapters 9-13

18. What announcement did Alfred make at breakfast to explain why he appeared to be "drunk"?
    A. He announced that he was in love.
    B. He explained that he was taking medication for allergies, and it made him appear drunk.
    C. He said he had been promoted at the store and would be making more money.
    D. He told his family about his boxing career.

19. What advice did Mr. Epstein give Alfred about boxing?
    A. He said Alfred should devote as much time as possible to it, that he was "a natural."
    B. He told Alfred not to let it interfere with his work, or he would be fired.
    C. He told Alfred to give it up because it was hard work, and one couldn't make an honest living at it because of the racketeers, and crooked mangers.
    D. He told Alfred to try it for six months, and then see if he still liked it. If he did, Mr. Epstein said he would buy Alfred some equipment and help him continue with his training.

20. Why did Alfred go to the clubroom?
    A. He wanted to see James, and he was frustrated with what he felt was a lack of progress in his boxing career.
    B. Major had told him that a girl he (Alfred) liked would be there. Alfred went to impress her with his muscles and fancy footwork.
    C. He went with the intention of beating up Major, but changed his mind.
    D. He wanted to try and convince the others to give up their non-productive ways and join the gym.

21. Which of the following did not happen at the clubroom?
    A. Alfred and James got into a fight.
    B. Alfred got drunk and passed out.
    C. Alfred tried to convince James to stop using drugs.
    D. Alfred and James left early and went to the gym.

22. True or False: Alfred went riding with Major, Hollis, and Sonny because he was feeling hung over, and the guys told him he needed a break from work. (Chapters 9-13)
    A. True
    B. False

23. Where did Alfred go after running away from the police?
    A. He went to the gym.
    B. He went to an art museum.
    C. He went for a run in the park.
    D. He went by the beach to the movies.

The Contender Multiple Choice Study/Quiz Questions Page 6

24. Where did Alfred go after work on Monday?
    A. He went to visit his aunt and uncle.
    B. He went to the clubroom.
    C. He went to the movies and then to clean out his locker at the gym.
    D. He went to his and James' secret hideout.

25. True or False: Mr. Donatelli encouraged Alfred to quit training. He said Alfred didn't have what it took to be a fighter.
    A. True
    B. False

26. How did Mr. Epstein show his renewed confidence in Alfred? (Chapters 9-13)
    A. He let Alfred carry the money to the bank on Friday evenings.
    B. He gave Alfred a raise.
    C. He said he would show Alfred how to work the register and add other, more responsible jobs.
    D. He gave Alfred a key to the store.

27. How did Alfred earn his mouthpiece?
    A. He hit the punching bag one hundred times in a row without stopping.
    B. He ran five miles a day for a week.
    C. He worked overtime at the store and Mr. Epstein paid for the mouthpiece
    D. He knocked down Jose in a sparring round.

The Contender Multiple Choice Study/Quiz Questions Page 7

<u>Chapters 14-16</u>

28. What did Charlene think Alfred was doing the next morning?
    A. She thought he had a hangover.
    B. She thought he was sick.
    C. She thought he was just being lazy and wanted her to wait on him.
    D. She thought he was depressed.

29. What had happened at the clubroom since Alfred was last there?
    A. It was raided by the police, who had found marijuana and heroin there.
    B. It had burned down when the boys got into a fight and accidentally tipped over a lit candle.
    C. The girls had fixed it up and cleaned.
    D. James had gotten drunk and destroyed most of the furniture. Now they were trying to repair it.

30. Spoon made an offer to Alfred. What was it?
    A. He offered to let Alfred move in with him.
    B. He offered to loan Alfred enough money to buy some good gym equipment.
    C. He offered to help Alfred find a night school when he would be ready to go back for his high school diploma.
    D. He offered to introduce Alfred to his younger sister.

31. True or False: When Jackson fell down and stayed down, Alfred thought Jackson just didn't want to get up. He didn't want to believe that Jackson was really hurt.
    A. True
    B. False

32. Did Alfred win his first fight? What was Mr. Donatelli's reaction?
    A. No, he didn't win. Mr. Donatelli said he didn't want it badly enough.
    B. Yes, he did win. Mr. Donatelli said that winning wasn't enough.
    C. No, he didn't win. Mr. Donatelli filed a complaint, saying the other fighter had cheated.
    D. Yes he did win. Mr. Donatelli praised him, and said he had done a great job.

33. Aunt Pearl, concerned for Alfred, lightly complained about his boxing. He replied, "I don't know about nothing else." What was her reply?
    A. She said, "Before the summer you didn't know about boxing neither."
    B. She said, "Your Mama didn't birth you to beat nobody up."
    C. She said, "Lord knows I done all I can. Now its up to you."
    D. She said, "If you hadn't a quit school like that, maybe you'd know something by now."

The Contender Multiple Choice Study/Quiz Questions Page 8

34. What did Alfred discover about his Aunt Pearl?
    A. She loved him as much as she loved her own children.
    B. She was even more stubborn than he had realized.
    C. She had once dreamed of being a singer, but never had the chance to reach for her dream.
    D. Her husband had been a boxer, and had died of a blow to the head. That was why she disliked boxing.

35. True or False: Alfred was satisfied with the result of his first fight, so he decided to quit.
    A. True
    B. False

36. Why did Alfred feel sick after his second fight?
    A. He had eaten his dinner too quickly, and too close to fight time. It made him feel sluggish and sick.
    B. He knocked out Griffin. The thought that he could have really hurt or killed his opponent made him sick.
    C. Dr. Corey had given him an injection of steroids, and he had an adverse reaction to them.
    D. He couldn't block out the jeers and taunts from the crowd, and hearing their insults demoralized him.

37. What happened when Alfred went back to the store the next day?
    A. Mr. Epstein gave him a raise.
    B. Mr. Epstein gave him the day off to rest and take some time for himself.
    C. There was a big banner in the window that said "Congratulations, Alfred".
    D. Nothing. Mr. Epstein acted like he didn't know anything about the fight.

38. For what volunteer job did Lynn and Harold try to recruit Alfred?
    A. They wanted him to be a bodyguard for older women who needed an escort to the bank when they cashed their Social Security checks.
    B. They wanted him to ask Mr. Epstein to donate food to the hungry.
    C. They wanted him to talk to the other gang members and ask them to leave the little children alone.
    D. They wanted him to help in their new neighborhood recreation program.

39. What did Alfred do on his afternoon off?
    A. He went home and slept.
    B. He walked the streets, looking for James.
    C. He worked at the gym.
    D. He went to the library to read about famous boxers.

The Contender Multiple Choice Study/Quiz Questions Page 9

Chapters 17-20

40. How did Uncle Wilson view Alfred's wins?
    A. He thought it was dangerous, that Alfred would just get his brains knocked out.
    B. He said top fighters could make contact with big people and get opportunities.
    C. He thought it was a good outlet for a boy of Alfred's limited talents.
    D. He was proud; he had always wanted to be a boxer, but was never good enough.

41. Alfred came to a decision that surprised Aunt Pearl. What was it?
    A. He said he was going to move out and get an apartment with Henry.
    B. He said he was going to quit working at Epstein's and get a job at one of the larger supermarket chains.
    C. He said he was going to devote himself full-time to boxing.
    D. He said he was going to go back to night school and get his high school diploma.

42. Who was the shuddering old man who crouched along side Alfred's stairs?
    A. It was James, looking for drug money.
    B. It was one of Donatelli's former pupils, warning Alfred that he could end up on the street, too.
    C. It was no one special, just a homeless drunk. The encounter made Alfred realize what a good life he had.
    D. It was Henry's grandfather. He was ill, and sometimes wandered the streets. Alfred took him back home.

43. What did Mr. Donatelli tell Alfred after his third fight?
    A. Mr. Donatelli told Alfred he was moving up to the next league so that he could fight more experienced boxers.
    B. Mr. Donatelli told Alfred he was opening a joint savings account with both of their names, and he would deposit Alfred's prize money.
    C. Mr. Donatelli told him it was time to retire because he didn't have the killer instinct.
    D. Mr. Donatelli told him if he finishes high school, he could probably get an athletic scholarship to a college.

44. True or False: Mr. Donatelli refused to let Alfred go one more fight. He didn't want to be embarrassed by Alfred's failure.
    A. True
    B. False

45. Why were the police looking for James?
    A. He has killed someone in a drug-induced rage.
    B. He had broken into Epstein's store again.
    C. He had been selling drugs to some of the children in the neighborhood.
    D. They wanted to question him about the whereabouts of Major and the others, who were suspected of robbing a bank.

The Contender Multiple Choice Study/Quiz Questions Page 10

46. What did Alfred do for James?
    A. He took him home, cleaned him up, and fed him.
    B. He turned him over to the police for his own good.
    C. He took him to a hospital and said he would help him get straight.
    D. He gave James enough money to last for a few weeks.

ANSWER KEY - MULTIPLE CHOICE STUDY/QUIZ QUESTIONS
The Contender

Chapters 1-4	Chapters 5-8	Chapters 9-13	Chapter 14-16
1. B	9. B	18. D	28. B
2. D	10. A	19. C	29. A
3. C	11. D	20. A	30. C
4. A	12. C	21. D	31. A
5. A	13. B	22. A	32. B
6. D	14. D	23. D	33. A
7. B	15. A	24. C	34. C
8. C	16. C	25. B	35. B
	17. B	26. C	36. B
		27. D	37. B
			38. D
			39. C

Chapters 17-20
40. B
41. D
42. A
43. C
44. B
45. B
46. C

PREREADING VOCABULARY WORKSHEETS

VOCABULARY - *The Contender*

Chapter 1 - 4 Part I: Using Prior Knowledge and Contextual Clues

Below are the sentences in which the vocabulary words appear in the text. Read the sentence. Use any clues you can find in the sentence combined with your prior knowledge, and write what you think the underlined words mean on the lines provided.

1. ...the perpetual grin spread across his skinny face.

   _____

2. ...the four of them were in a tight pile of swinging arms and legs, kicking, cuffing, punching, and Alfred smashed into the pavement.

   _____

3. Aunt Pearl waited until they had clattered out of the apartment and down the tenement stairs before...

   _____

4.-5. An occasional peal of drunken laughter drowned out the hoarse yells of tired children and the stoop chatter and the muted noise of a dozen transistors on different stations.

   _____

   _____

6. The nationalist on the stepladder...was whipping his growing audience out of its morning listlessness.

   _____

7. The serene look on Aunt Pearl's face calmed him at first, then made him angrier.

   _____

8. They lapsed into silence...

   _____

33

Contender Vocabulary Chapters 1-3 Continued

Part II: Determining the Meaning

You have tried to figure out the meanings of the vocabulary words for Chapter 1-4. Now match the vocabulary words to their dictionary definitions. If there are words for which you cannot figure out the definition by contextual clues and by process of elimination, look them up in a dictionary.

____ 1. perpetual   A. A loud burst of noise
____ 2. cuffing   B. Hum-drum; lifelessness; boredom
____ 3. tenement   C. Muffled; sound made soft by distance or interference
____ 4. peal   D. Passed; expired
____ 5. muted   E. Hitting with an open hand
____ 6. listlessness   F. Calm; unruffled
____ 7. serene   G. Continuing without interruption
____ 8. lapsed   H. A rundown, low-rent apartment building

Vocabulary - *The Contender*

Chapters 5-8 Part I: Using Prior Knowledge and Contextual Clues
 Below are the sentences in which the vocabulary words appear in the text. Read the sentence. Use any clues you can find in the sentence combined with your prior knowledge, and write what you think the underlined words mean on the lines provided.

1. In the ring, their heads <u>encased</u> by black leather guards, two fighters danced around each other...
   _____

2. ...Henry turned <u>impatiently</u>.
   _____

3. The sharpest of all were the big-time Harlem gamblers in white dinner jackets <u>elegantly</u> stepping with glittering women...
   _____

4. A <u>dignified</u> little man in a bright blue tuxedo climbed through the ropes...
   _____

5. The <u>preliminary</u> bouts were a blur of bodies and punches for Alfred...
   _____

6. The way he <u>concentrated</u> on protecting that eye left him wide open...
   _____

Part II: Determining the Meaning
 You have tried to figure out the meanings of the vocabulary words for Chapters 5-8. Now match the vocabulary words to their dictionary definitions. If there are words for which you cannot figure out the definition by contextual clues and by process of elimination, look them up in a dictionary.

___ 1. encased   A. That which goes before or prepares
___ 2. impatiently   B. Enclosed
___ 3. elegantly   C. With reserve; showing decorum; with dignity
___ 4. dignified   D. In a refined manner; classically beautifully
___ 5. preliminary   E. Diligently thought about; focused
___ 6. concentrated   F. Restlessly; anxiously

Vocabulary - *The Contender*

<u>Chapters 9-13</u> Part I: Using Prior Knowledge and Contextual Clues

    Below are the sentences in which the vocabulary words appear in the text. Read the sentence. Use any clues you can find in the sentence combined with your prior knowledge, and write what you think the underlined words mean on the lines provided.

1. This is a passing phase. He'll soon grow tired of this meaningless <u>pursuit</u> and devote his...

   _____

2. Willie Streeter came back to the gym, <u>sullen</u> and overweight.

   _____

3. The music was low, <u>funky</u> blues, and he swayed to it.

   _____

4. <u>Vaguely</u> he remembered that he had to call Dorothy about something...

   _____

5. While he was slipping them on, the car <u>veered</u> toward a young couple crossing the street.

   _____

6. Alfred began to feel cramps in his stomach at the <u>mingled</u> smells of cotton candy, barbecue, fried chicken, and hot dogs.

   _____

7. Alfred <u>vaulted</u> over the door, into the gutter, landing hard on his right foot.

   _____

8. He looked at the square head, <u>silhouetted</u> against the flickering neon lights.

   _____

Contender Vocabulary Chapters 9-13 Continued

Part II: Determining the Meaning

    You have tried to figure out the meanings of the vocabulary words for Chapters 9-13. Now match the vocabulary words to their dictionary definitions. If there are words for which you cannot figure out the definition by contextual clues and by process of elimination, look them up in a dictionary.

   ___ 1. pursuit   A. Seen as a dark outline against a light background
   ___ 2. sullen   B. Indistinctly; unclearly
   ___ 3. funky   C. Jumped
   ___ 4. vaguely   D. Activity engaged in regularly
   ___ 5. veered   E. Mixed
   ___ 6. mingled   F. Gloomy
   ___ 7. vaulted   G. Turned towards one side
   ___ 8. silhouetted   H. Earthy and uncomplicated; natural

Vocabulary - *The Contender*

Chapters 14-16 Part I: Using Prior Knowledge and Contextual Clues
    Below are the sentences in which the vocabulary words appear in the text. Read the sentence. Use any clues you can find in the sentence combined with your prior knowledge, and write what you think the underlined words mean on the lines provided.

1. ...the cab <u>lurched</u> into the uptown traffic.
_____

2. You get a Cadillac and a <u>chauffeur</u>?
_____

3. In these one-night <u>amateur</u> shows, the club in charge matches up the fighters at the last minute.
_____

4. The ice ball exploded, spraying his entire body with freezing, <u>paralyzing</u> streams of water, weighing down his arms, deadening his legs, squeezing his heart
_____

5. ...led them down a dark <u>corridor</u> into a large bare room.
_____

6. They stared at each other for a long time before Bud shook his head, and Donatelli <u>shrugged</u>.
_____

Part II: Determining the Meaning -- Match the vocabulary words to their definitions.

___ 1. lurched   A. Rolled or pitched suddenly or erratically
___ 2. chauffeur   B. Moved shoulders up and down as a gesture of doubt or
                        indifference
___ 3. amateur   C. Hallway
___ 4. corridor   D. Making unable to move or act
___ 5. paralyzing   E. A person who does an activity as a hobby instead of for pay
___ 6. shrugged   F. One employed to drive an automobile

Vocabulary - *The Contender*

<u>Chapters 17-20</u> Part I: Using Prior Knowledge and Contextual Clues

Below are the sentences in which the vocabulary words appear in the text. Read the sentence. Use any clues you can find in the sentence combined with your prior knowledge, and write what you think the underlined words mean on the lines provided.

1. "Are you guys <u>hypnotized</u>?"
_____

2. Even after an <u>addict</u> takes a cure, he needs a great deal of encouragement to stay off drugs.
_____

3. ...flexing his forearm muscles so the Marine Corps <u>emblem</u> jumped on the smooth bronze skin.
_____

4. Hubbard was <u>pummeling</u> his ribs now...
_____

Part II: Determining the Meaning

You have tried to figure out the meanings of the vocabulary words for Chapters 17-20. Now match the vocabulary words to their dictionary definitions. If there are words for which you cannot figure out the definition by contextual clues and by process of elimination, look them up in a dictionary.

___ 1. hypnotized   A. Dependent on a habit-forming substance
___ 2. addict   B. Beating with fists
___ 3. emblem   C. In a trance
___ 4. pummeling   D. Insignia; symbolic badge or design

ANSWER KEY - VOCABULARY - *The Contender*

Chapters 1-4	Chapters 5-8	Chapters 9-13	Chapters 14-16
1. G	1. B	1. D	1. A
2. E	2. F	2. F	2. F
3. H	3. D	3. H	3. E
4. A	4. C	4. B	4. C
5. C	5. A	5. G	5. D
6. B	6. E	6. E	6. B
7. F		7. C	
8. D		8. A	

Chapters 17-20
1. C
2. A
3. D
4. B

DAILY LESSONS

LESSON ONE

Objectives
    1. To introduce the *Contender* unit.
    2. To distribute books and other related materials
    3. To preview the study questions for chapters 1-4
    4. To familiarize students with the vocabulary for chapters 1-4

NOTE: You need to have students bring in pictures of something that represents a dream of something they would like to be or do or have in the future, something that represents their "dreams."
    Also in preparation, you need to put up the background paper and title for a bulletin board entitled I HAVE A DREAM or some other suitable phrase. Leave space for students to post their pictures.

Activity #1
    Ask students to clear their desks except for the pictures they have brought to class. Have each student explain what his/her picture represents and then let the student post it on the bulletin board.

TRANSITION: Explain that you are about to read *The Contender*, a story about a young man from Harlem who decided to try to achieve his dream.

Activity #2
    Distribute the materials students will use in this unit. Explain in detail how students are to use these materials.

    Study Guides Students should read the study guide questions for each reading assignment prior to beginning the reading assignment to get a feeling for what events and ideas are important in the section they are about to read. After reading the section, students will (as a class or individually) answer the questions to review the important events and ideas from that section of the book. Students should keep the study guides as study materials for the unit test.

    Vocabulary Prior to reading a reading assignment, students will do vocabulary work related to the section of the book they are about to read. Following the completion of the reading of the book, there will be a vocabulary review of all the words used in the vocabulary assignments. Students should keep their vocabulary work as study materials for the unit test.

    Reading Assignment Sheet You need to fill in the reading assignment sheet to let students know by when their reading has to be completed. You can either write the assignment sheet up on a side blackboard or bulletin board and leave it there for students to see each day, or you can "ditto" copies for each student to have. In either case, you should advise students to become very familiar with the reading assignments so they know what is expected of them.

Extra Activities Center   The unit resource portion of this unit contains suggestions for an extra library of related books and articles in your classroom as well as crossword and word search puzzles. Make an extra activities center in your room where you will keep these materials for students to use. (Bring the books and articles in from the library and keep several copies of the puzzles on hand.) Explain to students that these materials are available for students to use when they finish reading assignments or other class work early.

Nonfiction Assignment Sheet   Explain to students that they each are to read at least one non-fiction piece from the in-class library at some time during the unit. Students will fill out a nonfiction assignment sheet after completing the reading to help you evaluate their reading experiences and to help the students think about and evaluate their own reading experiences.

Books   Each school has its own rules and regulations regarding student use of school books. Advise students of the procedures that are normal for your school.

Activity #3
Preview the study questions and have students do the vocabulary work for Chapters 1-4 of *The Contender*. If students do not finish this assignment during this class period, they should complete it prior to the next class meeting.

NONFICTION ASSIGNMENT SHEET - *The Contender*
(To be completed after reading the required nonfiction article)

Name _____ Date _____

Title of Nonfiction Read _____

Written By _____ Publication Date _____

I. Factual Summary: Write a short summary of the piece you read.

II. Vocabulary
    1. With which vocabulary words in the piece did you encounter some degree of difficulty?

    2. How did you resolve your lack of understanding with these words?

III. Interpretation: What was the main point the author wanted you to get from reading his work?

IV. Criticism
    1. With which points of the piece did you agree or find easy to accept? Why?

    2. With which points of the piece did you disagree or find difficult to believe? Why?

V. Personal Response: What do you think about this piece? OR How does this piece influence your ideas?

LESSON TWO

Objectives
1. To read chapters 1-4
2. To give students practice reading orally
3. To evaluate students' oral reading

Activity

Have students read chapters 1-4 of *Contender* out loud in class. You probably know the best way to get readers with your class; pick students at random, ask for volunteers, or use whatever method works best for your group. If you have not yet completed an oral reading evaluation for your students this marking period, this would be a good opportunity to do so. A form is included with this unit for your convenience. If students do not complete reading chapters 1-4 in class, they should do so prior to your next class meeting.

LESSON THREE

Objectives
1. To review the main events and ideas from chapters 1-4
2. To preview the study questions for chapters 5-8
3. To familiarize students with the vocabulary in chapters 5-8
4. To read chapters 5-8

Activity #1

Give students a few minutes to formulate answers for the study guide questions for chapters 1-4, and then discuss the answers to the questions in detail. Write the answers on the board or overhead transparency so students can have the correct answers for study purposes.

Note: It is a good practice in public speaking and leadership skills for individual students to take charge of leading the discussions of the study questions. Perhaps a different student could go to the front of the class and lead the discussion each day that the study questions are discussed during this unit. Of course, the teacher should guide the discussion when appropriate and be sure to fill in any gaps the students leave.

Activity #2

Give students about fifteen minutes to preview the study questions for chapters 5-8 of *The Contender* and to do the related vocabulary work.

Activity #3

Have students read chapters 5-8 orally in class. If you are doing the oral reading evaluations, continue reading as in Lesson Two. If you are not officially evaluating oral reading, let students try partner reading: pair your students and let them take turns reading to each other. The non-reading partner should follow along in the book. If students do not complete the reading in class, they should do so prior to your next class meeting.

ORAL READING EVALUATION - *The Contender*

Name _____ Class _____ Date _____

SKILL	EXCELLENT	GOOD	AVERAGE	FAIR	POOR
Fluency	5	4	3	2	1
Clarity	5	4	3	2	1
Audibility	5	4	3	2	1
Pronunciation	5	4	3	2	1
_____	5	4	3	2	1
_____	5	4	3	2	1

Total _____ Grade _____

Comments:

LESSON FOUR

Objectives
1. To check to see that students read chapters 5-8 as assigned
2. To review the main ideas and events from chapters 5-8
3. To give students the opportunity to practice writing to express their own opinions
4. To give the teacher the opportunity to evaluate students' writing skills
5. To have students think about what it means to be a "contender"
6. To have students make the association between an idea in a book and real life

Activity #1
Quiz - Distribute quizzes and give students about 10 minutes to complete them. (Note: The quizzes may either be the short answer study guides or the multiple choice version for chapters 5-8.) Have students exchange papers. Grade the quizzes as a class. Collect the papers for recording the grades.

Activity #2
Distribute Writing Assignment #1. Discuss the directions in detail and give students ample time to complete the assignment.

Follow - Up: After you have graded the assignments, have a writing conference with the students. (This unit schedules one in Lesson Twelve.) After the writing conference, allow students to revise their papers using your suggestions and corrections. Give them about three days from the date they receive their papers to complete the revision. Grading the revisions on an A-C-E scale (all revisions well-done, some revisions made, few or no revisions made) will speed your grading time and still give some credit for the students' efforts.

LESSON FIVE

Objectives
1. To preview the vocabulary and study questions for chapters 9-13
2. To read chapters 9-13

Activity #1
Give students ten to fifteen minutes to preview the study questions and do the prereading vocabulary work for chapters 9-13.

Activity #2
Tell students that prior to your next class meeting they should have completed reading chapters 9-13. Students may use the remainder of this class time to work on this assignment. If you have not completed the oral reading evaluations, do so during this class period. If you have completed them, students may use this time to read silently.

WRITING ASSIGNMENT #1 - *The Contender*

PROMPT
Alfred decided to become a contender, to work towards his goal, to be involved with the direction of his own life. Your assignment is to answer the question, "Are you a contender?" Your composition should thoroughly explain your reasons for thinking you either are or are not a contender.

PREWRITING
One way to begin is to think about the question and answer it honestly. Jot down the reasons why you came to the conclusion you did. Give examples of the characteristics you attribute to yourself to support your claims.

DRAFTING
Write a paragraph in which you introduce the idea that you are (or are not) a contender.

The body of your composition should be composed of several paragraphs, one paragraph for each reason you think you are (or are not) a contender. These paragraphs will be filled out with the examples you have chosen to support your claims.

Write a concluding paragraph summarizing your points and stating whether or not you are satisfied with being (or not being) a contender. (Would you want to change?)

PROMPT
When you finish the rough draft of your paper, ask a student who sits near you to read it. After reading your rough draft, he/she should tell you what he/she liked best about your work, which parts were difficult to understand, and ways in which your work could be improved. Reread your paper considering your critic's comments, and make the corrections you think are necessary.

PROOFREADING
Do a final proofreading of your paper double-checking your grammar, spelling, organization, and the clarity of your ideas.

LESSON SIX

Objectives
    1. To review the main ideas of chapters 9-13
    2. To evaluate students' use and understanding of grammar
    3. To review a few basic rules of grammar

Activity #1
    Ask students to get out their books and some paper (not their study guides). Tell students to write down ten questions (and answers) which cover the main events and ideas in chapters 9-13.
    Discuss the students questions and answers orally, making a list of the questions with brief responses on the board. Put a star next to the students' questions and answers that are essentially the same as the study guide questions. (Be sure that all the study guide questions are answered.)

Activity #2
    Distribute the Grammar Worksheet. Discuss the directions in detail and give students ample time to complete the assignment. After students have completed the worksheet, discuss the corrections students made. Have students explain why they made the corrections they did make. Discuss the appropriate rules of grammar.

LESSON SEVEN

Objectives
    1. To preview the study questions and vocabulary for chapters 14-16
    2. To read chapters 14-16

Activity #1
    Give students ten or fifteen minutes to preview the study questions for chapters 14-16 and to do the related prereading vocabulary work.

Activity #2
    Tell students that prior to your next class meeting they must have completed reading chapters 14-16. Students may have the remainder of this period to work on this assignment.

GRAMMAR WORKSHEET - *The Contender*

Correct the errors in the following passages, and be prepared to explain the changes you make:

1. I ain't gonna press you, Alfred, you do a man's work and I ain't gonna treat you like a boy.

2. Alfred, . . . you wasn't really fixin' to go with James that night . . . Alfred!

3. I got doctors call me from California ask what's in it.

4. Ever since you come . . . you been a smart meat.

5. I say you ain't no man, neither.

6. Figured. Tonight you gonna see a real fight, no slappin'.

7. You got to Thursday to decide.

8. He no wear your trunks, Petey.

9. He too fat.

10. I been 'round.
    Never called or nothing.

11. What you got to say?

12. Ocean air, champ, best thing for you.

Contender Grammar Worksheet Page 2

13. Loaned it off a guy.

14. Got no change, Major.

15. Let's get out a here.

16. Brooksy, hey, Brooksy, wanna talk to you.

17. Listen, man, I don't think there's gonna be no trouble, but if anybody asks where you was today, we all was over your house playin' cards.

18. I do it so he feel good.

19. Nex' time he feel so good he knock you out.

20. You been taking a little step before you threw the hook, made you off balance.

21. Ain't you gonna run this morning?

22. Knee bends, that's it, go on down, bounce up, that's the way.

23. Rivera was already out there, planted and ready, stick and run, Alfred, stick and run. He darted in, pop-pop, danced back, in and out, in and out, jab and duck, hit and move, circle left, pop-pop, circle right, pop-pop, and he could feel Rivera's blow-torch breaths, hot and heavy against his chest.

24. Thunk. Lucky punch, beautiful hook. Pitter-pat. NO SALE. pop-pop-pop, and there was Rivera, and the crowd was screaming, get in there and fight, black boy, coward.

LESSON EIGHT

<u>Objectives</u>
1. To review the main ideas and events in chapters 14-16
2. To preview the study questions and vocabulary for chapters 17-20
3. To read chapters 17-20

<u>Activity #1</u>
Give students a few minutes to formulate answers to the study questions for chapters 14-16. Discuss the answers to the questions in detail.

<u>Activity #2</u>
Divide your class into groups of five students. Have students take turns reading orally within their groups. When students are not reading orally, they should follow along in their books with the students who are reading.

LESSONS NINE AND TEN

<u>Objectives</u>
1. To review the main ideas and events from chapters 17-20
2. To discuss *The Contender* on interpretive and critical levels

<u>Activity #1</u>
Take a few minutes at the beginning of the period to review the study questions for chapters 17-20.

<u>Activity #2</u>
Choose the questions from the Extra Discussion Questions/Writing Assignments which seem most appropriate for your students. A class discussion of these questions is most effective if students have been given the opportunity to formulate answers to the questions prior to the discussion. To this end, you may either have all the students formulate answers to all the questions, divide your class into groups and assign one or more questions to each group, or you could assign one question to each student in your class. The option you choose will make a difference in the amount of class time needed for this activity.

<u>Activity #3</u>
After students have had ample time to formulate answers to the questions, begin your class discussion of the questions and the ideas presented by the questions. Be sure students take notes during the discussion so they have information to study for the unit test.

EXTRA WRITING ASSIGNMENTS/DISCUSSION QUESTIONS - *Contender*

Interpretation

1. From what point of view is *The Contender* written? What does the author gain by using this viewpoint?

2. If you were to rewrite *The Contender* as a play, where would you start and end each act? Explain why.

3. Where is the climax of the story?

4. What are the main conflicts in the story and if they are resolved, how are they resolved?

5. Explain how the title of the book is appropriate.

6. At what times did Alfred go to the movies? Why?

Critical

6. Explain Henry's role in the story.

7. Are Alfred's actions believably motivated? Explain why or why not.

8. Explain the importance of the setting in *The Contender*. Could this story have been set in a different time and place and still have the same effect?

9. Characterize Robert Lipsyte's style of writing. How does it contribute to the value of the novel?

10. Compare and contrast Alfred and James.

11. Explain the influences of these people on Alfred: Henry, Donatelli, Epstein, Spoon, Aunt Pearl, James.

12. This book has a variety of character types. Make a list of the characters, describe their "types," and explain the use of each character in the book.

13. Alfred passes through several stages in the book. Define the stages he passes through as his character develops. Use examples from the book.

14. Other people give their opinions about Alfred during the book. Who says what about him? What is the cumulative effect of these comments?

Contender Extra Discussion Questions page 2

15. Time is a factor in the story. Find all the references to it you can in the text. Explain the importance of "time" in the story.

16. Several times in the story, people and situations aren't what they appear to be. Find them in the text. Why were they included?

17. When and why does Alfred hide from Henry?

18. Why is the fact that Henry bought Alfred's robe symbolically important?

19. What are Alfred's strengths? Weaknesses?

20. Black and white, dark and light images appear throughout the book. Find the references to these and explain how they are used.

21. What activities in the book are presented as being positive things? What things are negative?

22. Is the "nationalist rally" presented as being positive or negative? Why?

23. Is *The Contender* a tragedy? If so, how? If not, why not?

Personal Response

24. Did you enjoy reading *The Contender*? Why or why not?

25. Were the boys at the clubroom "bad"? Define "bad."

26. What faults in our society does Robert Lipsyte point out in *The Contender*?

27. Donatelli says, "Everyone is somebody." Define "somebody."

28. What will James and Alfred be doing 10 years after the end of the story?

29. Why did Donatelli stay in the boxing business?

30. How do sports contribute to a person's character?

31. In what ways, if any, are sports bad for a person?

32. Who are your heroes? Why?

Contender Quotations/ Extra Discussion Questions Page 3

Quotations

1. The, uh, old stone fence off Lenox, Aunt Pearl. I was walking on it, and . . . a . . . a big dog jumped up. Knocked me off." (Alfred, Ch.2)

2. Stay in bed, man, curl up like a baby, close your eyes, make the world go away." (Alfred, Ch.2)

3. A man must have some fear. (Donatelli, Ch.3)

4. People will try to drag you down. (Donatelli, Ch.3)

5. Everybody is somebody. (Donatelli, Ch.3)

6. You have to start by wanting to be a contender, the man coming up, the man who knows there's a good chance he'll never get to the top, the man who's willing to sweat and bleed to get up as high as his legs and his brains and his heart will take him. (Donatelli, Ch.3)

7. It's the climbing that makes the man. Getting to the top is an extra reward. (Donatelli, Ch.3)

8. And nothing's promised you, nothing's ever promised you. (Donatelli, Ch.3)

9. They'll be more places for colored people soon. But you have to be ready, have to have your education. Have to be qualified. (Wilson, Ch.4)

Contender Quotations/ Extra Discussion Questions Page 4

10. He's got his foot on your throat, you gonna lick his shoe? Come march with us, Alfred. Maybe later, Happy little darky. World is opening up for colored people. Devil's got new uniforms. We'll get you. Everybody wants to be a champion, Alfred. Slave. Nothing's promised you. Slave. Opportunity for advancement? You have to start by wanting to be a contender. (Alfred, Ch.4)

11. You're a good boy, Alfred, we all think you're a good boy. I told the police not to bother you. But sometimes it's hard to . . . well, we trust you, but for your own sake there's no point tempting fate. You understand. (Epstein, Ch.5)

12. James turned and swaggered away. Like Major. (Alfred, Ch.5)

13. Hold it right there, said the cop. Slave, said Major. Good boy, said Lou. (Alfred, Ch.5)

14. Alfred felt in his pocket. Enough for a nice dark movie, he thought, sit and watch it forever. (Ch.5)

15. But Willie knows how, and there's a difference right there. (Bud, Ch.6)

16. Don't nobody tell the boss about this. Everybody gets a second chance around here. (Bud, Ch.6)

17. . . . and all the way home he wanted to raise his right arm to the ringside crowd on the stoops. (Alfred, Ch. 8)

18. Hang in there, Al, you're lookin' good. (Policeman, Ch.9)

Contender Quotations/ Extra Discussion Questions Page 5

19. Not like the old days when Alfred would follow James up to a corner of the balcony and root for the monster and cheer the Indians and afterward change the ending of the picture if they didn't like how it came out. (Alfred, Ch. 10)

20. Then they all disappeared and left him alone, lying on the linoleum kitchen floor in a pool of ice-cold sweat. (Ch. 12)

21. A junkie tryin' to beat it with food, just can't do it, you just can't . . . (Passer-by, Ch.12)

22. He found a feature up on 125th Street, and went in. He had seen all the pictures on television already. So what. See them again, see them a thousand times, the new ones are the same as the old ones anyway. (Alfred, Ch.12)

23. Get up, go to work, go home and sleep so you can work some more and pay for your fun on the weekend. And then it's Monday again. Days move so slow. (Alfred, Ch.12)

24. You should have your own mind, do what you want. (Epstein, Ch.13)

25. He just didn't want to get back up. (Alfred, Ch.14)

26. Before the summer you didn't know about boxing neither. (Pearl, Ch.15)

27. But you would of liked to try. (Alfred to Pearl, Ch.15)

28. At least you've done something. (Lynn, Ch.16)

29. Always got to be planning for the future, thinking ahead. Wake up one morning and you find the world passed you by. (Wilson, Ch. 17)

30. Times are really changing. (Wilson, Ch. 17)

LESSONS ELEVEN AND TWELVE

Objectives
1. To relate the book to students' own lives
2. To show students the importance of having goals and plans
3. To have students practice setting goals and making a plan as to how to achieve them

NOTE: Prior to this lesson, you need to have invited a guest speaker to come to your class to discuss the importance of setting goals and making plans. A speaker from outside of your school would be best -- a psychologist, business personnel manager, trainer of sales people, etc. -- but if you cannot find anyone in your community willing to come, ask the people in your guidance office to make a short presentation.

Activity #1
Introduce the idea that Alfred set a goal for himself and worked towards it and that goals are important in all of our lives. Introduce your guest speaker and give him/her ample time to make a presentation about this topic to your students. Any information the speaker could give about the importance of setting goals and making plans, and ways to go about doing it would be appreciated.

Activity #2.
Distribute Writing Assignment #2. Discuss the directions in detail and give students ample time to complete the assignment.

NOTE: While students are working on their writing assignments, call individual students to your desk or some other private area for individual writing conferences based on the first writing assignment for this unit. A Writing Evaluation Form is included with this unit for your convenience if you would like to use it to help structure your conferences. All students should revise their first writing assignments based upon your comments and the conference. Tell students when these revisions will be due.

WRITING ASSIGNMENT #2 - *The Contender*

PROMPT
In the story *The Contender*, Alfred decided upon his goal, to be a boxer, a contender, eventually a champion. Mr. Donatelli told Alfred what would be required of him: certain eating and exercising requirements, times of frustration, times when he would be alone in his pursuit.

Your assignment is to make a goal for yourself and make a plan of action which will help you to achieve that goal.

PREWRITNG
Answer these prompts on a separate sheet of paper:
1. My goal is:
2. The steps I need to take to achieve that goal are:
3. Problems I could encounter which might keep me from achieving my goal are:
4. I can overcome these problems by:
5. I am motivated to achieve my goal because:
6. I do/don't think I will reach my goal because:

DRAFTING
After you have answered these prompts, begin to write your assignment into paragraph form. Use the worksheet as a general guide to organize your paragraphs. Write at least one good paragraph for each of the prompts above.

PROMPT
When you finish the rough draft of your paper, ask a student who sits near you to read it. After reading your rough draft, he/she should tell you what he/she liked best about your work, which parts were difficult to understand, and ways in which your work could be improved. Reread your paper considering your critic's comments, and make the corrections you think are necessary.

PROOFREADING
Do a final proofreading of your paper double-checking your grammar, spelling, organization, and the clarity of your ideas.

WRITING EVALUATION FORM - *The Contender*

Name _____ Date _____

Writing Assignment #1 for the *Contender* unit   Grade _____

Circle One For Each Item:

Grammar: excellent   good   fair   poor

Spelling: excellent   good   fair   poor

Punctuation: excellent   good   fair   poor

Legibility: excellent   good   fair   poor

Strengths:

Weaknesses:

Comments/Suggestions:

LESSON THIRTEEN

Objective
   To review all of the vocabulary work done in this unit

Activity
   Choose one (or more) of the vocabulary review activities listed below and spend your class period as directed in the activity. Some of the materials for these review activities are located in the Vocabulary Resource section of this unit.

VOCABULARY REVIEW ACTIVITIES

1. Divide your class into two teams and have an old-fashioned spelling or definition bee.

2. Give each of your students (or students in groups of two, three or four) a *Contender* Vocabulary Word Search Puzzle. The person (group) to find all of the vocabulary words in the puzzle first wins.

3. Give students a *Contender* Vocabulary Word Search Puzzle without the word list. The person or group to find the most vocabulary words in the puzzle wins.

4. Use a *Contender* Vocabulary Crossword Puzzle. Put the puzzle onto a transparency on the overhead projector (so everyone can see it), and do the puzzle together as a class.

5. Give students a *Contender* Vocabulary Matching Worksheet to do.

6. Divide your class into two teams. Use the *Contender* vocabulary words with their letters jumbled as a word list. Student 1 from Team A faces off against Student 1 from Team B. You write the first jumbled word on the board. The first student (1A or 1B) to unscramble the word wins the chance for his/her team to score points. If 1A wins the jumble, go to student 2A and give him/her a definition. He/she must give you the correct spelling of the vocabulary word which fits that definition. If he/she does, Team A scores a point, and you give student 3A a definition for which you expect a correctly spelled matching vocabulary word. Continue giving Team A definitions until some team member makes an incorrect response. An incorrect response sends the game back to the jumbled-word face off, this time with students 2A and 2B. Instead of repeating giving definitions to the first few students of each team, continue with the student after the one who gave the last incorrect response on the team. For example, if Team B wins the jumbled-word face-off, and student 5B gave the last incorrect answer for Team B, you would start this round of definition questions with student 6B, and so on. The team with the most points wins!

7. Have students write a story in which they correctly use as many vocabulary words as possible. Have students read their compositions orally! Post the most original compositions on your bulletin board!

LESSONS FOURTEEN AND FIFTEEN

Objectives
1. To widen the breadth of students' knowledge about the topics discussed or touched upon in *The Contender*
2. To check students' nonfiction reading assignments

Activity #1

Take students to the library so they can find nonfiction information to read relating to *The Contender* to fulfill their nonfiction reading assignment. Give students time to find their articles and read them in Lesson Fourteen.

Activity #2

In Lesson Fifteen ask each student to give a brief oral report about the nonfiction work he/she read for the nonfiction reading assignment. Your criteria for evaluating this report will vary depending on the level of your students. You may wish for students to give a complete report without using notes of any kind, or you may want students to read directly from a written report, or you may want to do something in between these two extremes. Just make students aware of your criteria in ample time for them to prepare their reports.

Start with one student's report. After that, ask if anyone else in the class has read about a topic related to the first student's report. If no one has, choose another student at random. After each report, be sure to ask if anyone has a report related to the one just completed. That will help keep a continuity during the discussion of the reports.

LESSON SIXTEEN

Objectives
1. To give students the opportunity to practice writing to persuade
2. To review characters and their motivations
3. To give the teacher a chance to evaluate students' individual writing

Activity

Distribute Writing Assignment #2. Discuss the directions orally in detail. Allow the remaining class time for students to complete the activity.

If students do not have enough class time to finish, the papers may be collected at the beginning of the next class period.

Follow-Up: Follow up as in Writing Assignment 1, allowing students to correct their errors and turn in the revision for credit. A good time for your next writing conferences would be the day following the unit test.

WRITING ASSIGNMENT #3 - *The Contender*

PROMPT

James and Alfred were good friends in the beginning of the book. Shortly after the book begins, they are separated. At that point, they begin to take different routes in life. Alfred decides to become a contender, and James chooses the life of crime and drugs. In the end of the book, however, Alfred's strengths come through, and he is determined to help James become a contender, too.

Suppose, though, that Alfred had been able to get through to James earlier in the book. James may never have sunk as low as he did. Your assignment is to choose a point in time in the book when you believe Alfred would have had the best chance of convincing James to become a contender, and write a scene in which Alfred persuades James to *become* a contender.

PREWRITING

First, decide at what point in the book Alfred would most likely have been able to convert James.

Next, how would Alfred convince James to become a contender, to take responsibility for the direction of his own life? Where would he choose to do it? What arguments would he use? What would he say?

Bearing this in mind, jot down a few notes about what James' reaction would have been. If it would be negative, how would Alfred overcome his friend's resistance?

Make notes about how you think the conversation would have gone. There does not have to be an immediate conclusion as to whether or not James is convinced, but you may make him either convinced or not convinced if you choose. The important part is to put forth a believable, persuasive argument, recognize that James will probably have objections, and find a way to overcome those objections.

DRAFTING

In the first paragraph of your composition, set the scene. Tell your reader at what point in the book your action will take place.

Write your scene. Use your book as a pattern for punctuation and capitalization in dialogue.

PROOFREADING

When you finish the rough draft of your paper, ask a student who sits near you to read it. After reading your rough draft, he/she should tell you what he/she liked best about your work, which parts were difficult to understand, and ways in which your work could be improved. Reread your paper considering your critic's comments, and make the corrections you think are necessary. Do a final proofreading of your paper double-checking your grammar, spelling, organization, and the clarity of your ideas.

LESSON SEVENTEEN

Objective
    To review the main ideas presented in *The Contender*

Activity #1
    Choose one of the review games/activities included in this unit and spend your class period as outlined there. Some materials for these activities are located in the Unit Resource section of this unit.

Activity #2
    Remind students that the Unit Test will be in the next class meeting. Stress the review of the Study Guides and their class notes as a last minute, brush-up review for homework.

REVIEW GAMES/ACTIVITIES - *The Contender*

1. Ask the class to make up a unit test for *The Contender*. The test should have 4 sections: matching, true/false, short answer, and essay. Students may use 1/2 period to make the test and then swap papers and use the other 1/2 class period to take a test a classmate has devised. (open book) You may want to use the unit test included in this unit or take questions from the students' unit tests to formulate your own test.

2. Take 1/2 period for students to make up true and false questions (including the answers). Collect the papers and divide the class into two teams. Draw a big tic-tac-toe board on the chalk board. Make one team X and one team O. Ask questions to each side, giving each student one turn. If the question is answered correctly, that students' team's letter (X or O) is placed in the box. If the answer is incorrect, no mark is placed in the box. The object is to get three marks in a row like tic-tac-toe. You may want to keep track of the number of games won for each team.

3. Take 1/2 period for students to make up questions (true/false and short answer). Collect the questions. Divide the class into two teams. You'll alternate asking questions to individual members of teams A & B (like in a spelling bee). The question keeps going from A to B until it is correctly answered, then a new question is asked. A correct answer does not allow the team to get another question. Correct answers are +2 points; incorrect answers are -1 point.

4. Have students pair up and quiz each other from their study guides and class notes.

5. Give students a *Contender* crossword puzzle to complete.

6. Divide your class into two teams. Use the *Contender* crossword words with their letters jumbled as a word list. Student 1 from Team A faces off against Student 1 from Team B. You write the first jumbled word on the board. The first student (1A or 1B) to unscramble the word wins the chance for his/her team to score points. If 1A wins the jumble, go to student 2A and give him/her a clue. He/she must give you the correct word which matches that clue. If he/she does, Team A scores a point, and you give student 3A a clue for which you expect another correct response. Continue giving Team A clues until some team member makes an incorrect response. An incorrect response sends the game back to the jumbled-word face off, this time with students 2A and 2B. Instead of repeating giving clues to the first few students of each team, continue with the student after the one who gave the last incorrect response on the team. For example, if Team B wins the jumbled-word face-off, and student 5B gave the last incorrect answer for Team B, you would start this round of clue questions with student 6B, and so on. The team with the most points wins!

UNIT TESTS

SHORT ANSWER UNIT TEST 1 - *The Contender*

I. Matching/Identify

___ 1. Jelly Belly   A. Handicapped trainer and friend to Alfred

___ 2. Alfred   B. Manager

___ 3. James   C. "Look for opportunities for the future"

___ 4. Spoon   D. Ex-fighter, Alfred's boss at work

___ 5. Henry   E. The "contender"

___ 6. Bud   F. Bully, gang-leader

___ 7. Aunt Pearl   G. Tried to recruit Alfred to nationalist rally

___ 8. Uncle Wilson   H. Raised Alfred

___ 9. Major   I. Best friend of Alfred

___ 10. Lynn   J. Lacked self-discipline with food

___ 11. Donatelli   K. Knocked out James

___ 12. Epstein   L. The cut-man; assistant manager

                            M. Ex-fighter, teacher

II. Short Answer

1. How is Alfred different from the other boys at the clubroom?

2. Why did Alfred first go to Donatelli's Gym?

3. Describe the relationship between James and Alfred.

Contender Short Answer Unit Test 1 Page 2

4. Why did Alfred stand up to Major? What was the result?

5. Why did Alfred go to the clubroom even though he was in training?

6. Why did Alfred return to training after "quitting"?

7. What was Spoon's offer to Alfred?

8. Aunt Pearl, concerned for Alfred, lightly complains about Alfred's boxing. He replies, "I don't know about nothing else." What is her response? What does she mean?

9. Why did Alfred feel sick after his second fight?

10. Who was the shuddering old man next to Alfred's stairs? What did he want?

Contender Short Answer Unit Test 1 Page 3

III. Essay

What are we supposed to learn from reading *The Contender*? Be specific and use examples from the text where appropriate.

Contender Short Answer Unit Test 1 Page 4

IV. Vocabulary

   Listen to the vocabulary words and spell them. After you have spelled all the words, go back and write down the definitions.

   1.

   2.

   3.

   4.

   5.

   6.

   7.

   8.

   9.

   10.

KEY: SHORT ANSWER UNIT TEST #1 - *The Contender*

I. Matching/Identify

_J_ 1. Jelly Belly   A. Handicapped trainer and friend to Alfred

_E_ 2. Alfred   B. Manager

_I_ 3. James   C. "Look for opportunities for the future"

_M_ 4. Spoon   D. Ex-fighter, Alfred's boss at work

_A_ 5. Henry   E. The "contender"

_L_ 6. Bud   F. Bully, gang-leader

_H_ 7. Aunt Pearl   G. Tried to recruit Alfred to nationalist rally

_C_ 8. Uncle Wilson   H. Raised Alfred

_F_ 9. Major   I. Best friend of Alfred

_G_ 10. Lynn   J. Lacked self-discipline with food

_B_ 11. Donatelli   K. Knocked out James

_D_ 12. Epstein   L. The cut-man; assistant manager

                                                            M. Ex-fighter, teacher

II. Short Answer

1. How is Alfred different from the other boys at the clubroom?
    He works and goes to church and tries to stay out of trouble.
2. Why did Alfred first go to Donatelli's Gym?
    He was tired of being afraid of stronger gang members, and he wanted to be a somebody, a champion.
3. Describe the relationship between James and Alfred.
    They were best friends as kids. They slowly grew apart in young adulthood. After James got caught for the robbery, they were very distant. Alfred missed his old friend but was not interested in joining in James' new lifestyle. In the end, their friendship endured as Alfred promised to help James get back on track.

4. Why did Alfred stand up to Major? What was the result?

    He had things he wanted to do and being involved with a crime would mess up his future, so he refused Major. Major backed down and had a new respect for Alfred.

5. Why did Alfred go to the clubroom even though he was in training?

    He wanted to see James, and he was frustrated with what he thought was a lack of progress with his boxing career.

6. Why did Alfred return to training after "quitting"?

    He didn't really want to quit in the first place; he was just frustrated and confused. His talk with Mr. Donatelli gave him enough hope to relieve his frustration. Also his days without training were slow and pointless.

7. What was Spoon's offer to Alfred?

    He said he and his wife would help Alfred find a school when he was ready to go back to classes for his high school diploma.

8. Aunt Pearl, concerned for Alfred, lightly complains about Alfred's boxing. He replies, "I don't know about nothing else." What is her response? What does she mean?

    She said, "Before the summer you didn't know about boxing neither." She meant that if he could learn to box, he could learn other things, too.

9. Why did Alfred feel sick after his second fight?

    He knocked out Griffin. He didn't want to hurt him. The thought that he could have really hurt him or killed him made him sick.

10. Who was the shuddering old man next to Alfred's stairs? What did he want?

    James was the man next to Alfred's stairs. He wanted money to buy drugs.

III. Essay answers will vary according to your class discussions and the students' opinions.

IV. Vocabulary - Choose ten of the vocabulary words. Read the words orally for students to write down. Students will go back later to fill in the appropriate definitions.

SHORT ANSWER UNIT TEST 2 - *The Contender*

I. Matching/Identify

___ 1. Jelly Belly   A. Manager

___ 2. Alfred   B. Best friend of Alfred

___ 3. James   C. Tried to recruit Alfred to nationalist rally

___ 4. Spoon   D. The "contender"

___ 5. Henry   E. Bully, gang-leader

___ 6. Bud   F. Ex-fighter, Alfred's boss at work

___ 7. Aunt Pearl   G. Raised Alfred

___ 8. Uncle Wilson   H. "Look for opportunities for the future"

___ 9. Major   I. Lacked self-discipline with food

___ 10. Lynn   J. Ex-fighter, teacher

___ 11. Donatelli   K. The cut-man; assistant manager

___ 12. Epstein   L. Knocked out James

                           M. Handicapped trainer and friend to Alfred

II. Short Answer

1. Why did Major, Hollis, and Sonny beat up Alfred?

2. Before he went to bed Sunday night, Alfred thought, ". . . Slave. Nothing's promised you. Slave. Opportunity for advancement? You have to start by wanting to be a contender." What did he decide?

Contender Short Answer Unit Test 2 Page 2

3. Describe the relationship between James and Alfred.

4. Why did Alfred go riding with Major, Hollis and Sonny?

5. Why did Alfred return to training after "quitting"?

6. What did Alfred discover he had in common with his aunt?

7. Why did Alfred feel sick after his second fight?

8. What did Alfred do for James?

Contender Short Answer Unit Test 2 Page 3

III. Quotations - Explain the importance or significance of each of the following quotes using examples from the book to illustrate your points:

1. People will try to drag you down. (Donatelli, Ch.3)

2. Everybody is somebody. (Donatelli, Ch.3)

3. It's the climbing that makes the man. Getting to the top is an extra reward. (Donatelli, Ch.3)

4. Alfred felt in his pocket. Enough for a nice dark movie, he thought, sit and watch it forever. (Ch.5)

5. Times are really changing. (Wilson, Ch. 17)

Contender Short Answer Unit Test 2 page 4

IV. Vocabulary

Listen to the vocabulary words and spell them. After you have spelled all the words, go back and write down the definitions.

1.

2.

3.

4.

5.

6.

7.

8.

9.

10.

KEY: SHORT ANSWER UNIT TEST 2 - *The Contender*

I. Matching (Use this matching key also for the Advanced Short Answer Unit Test)

__I__ 1. Jelly Belly   A. Manager

__D__ 2. Alfred   B. Best friend of Alfred

__B__ 3. James   C. Tried to recruit Alfred to nationalist rally

__J__ 4. Spoon   D. The "contender"

__M__ 5. Henry   E. Bully, gang-leader

__K__ 6. Bud   F. Ex-fighter, Alfred's boss at work

__G__ 7. Aunt Pearl   G. Raised Alfred

__H__ 8. Uncle Wilson   H. "Look for opportunities for the future"

__E__ 9. Major   I. Lacked self-discipline with food

__C__ 10. Lynn   J. Ex-fighter, teacher

__A__ 11. Donatelli   K. The cut-man; assistant manager

__F__ 12. Epstein   L. Knocked out James

                                         M. Handicapped trainer and friend to Alfred

II. Short Answer

1. Why did Major, Hollis, and Sonny beat up Alfred?
    Alfred forgot to tell them about the silent alarm, and because of that, they nearly got caught by the police.
2. Before he went to bed Sunday night, Alfred thought, ". . . Slave. Nothing's promised you. Slave. Opportunity for advancement? You have to start by wanting to be a contender." What did he decide?
    He decided to begin training, to be a contender.

3. Describe the relationship between James and Alfred.
>They were best friends as kids. They were slowly growing apart as young adults. After James got caught for the robbery, they were very distant. Alfred missed his old friend, but he was not interested in participating in James' new lifestyle of crime and drugs.

4. Why did Alfred go riding with Major, Hollis and Sonny?
>He was feeling hung-over, the guys told him he needed a break from work, and it was easier to go than to refuse.

5. Why did Alfred return to training after "quitting"?
>He didn't really want to quit in the first place; he was just frustrated and somewhat confused. His talk with Mr. Donatelli gave him enough hope to relieve his frustration. Also, his days without training were slow and pointless.

6. What did Alfred discover he had in common with his aunt?
>She had a dream once, too. Unlike Alfred, though, she never had the chance to reach for her dream.

7. Why did Alfred feel sick after his second fight?
>He knocked out Griffin. He didn't want to hurt him; the thought that he could have really hurt or killed him made him sick.

8. What did Alfred do for James?
>He found him at their "cave" and saved his life by convincing him to go to a hospital. From their conversation, one can assume that Alfred will do all he can to help James have a more meaningful life.

III. Quotations Responses will vary.

IV. Vocabulary
>Choose ten of the vocabulary words for part IV of the unit test. Read the words orally for students to write down and define.

ADVANCED SHORT ANSWER UNIT TEST - *The Contender*

I. Matching/Identify

___ 1. Jelly Belly   A. Manager

___ 2. Alfred   B. Best friend of Alfred

___ 3. James   C. Tried to recruit Alfred to nationalist rally

___ 4. Spoon   D. The "contender"

___ 5. Henry   E. Bully, gang-leader

___ 6. Bud   F. Ex-fighter, Alfred's boss at work

___ 7. Aunt Pearl   G. Raised Alfred

___ 8. Uncle Wilson   H. "Look for opportunities for the future"

___ 9. Major   I. Lacked self-discipline with food

___ 10. Lynn   J. Ex-fighter, teacher

___ 11. Donatelli   K. The cut-man; assistant manager

___ 12. Epstein   L. Knocked out James

                      M. Handicapped trainer and friend to Alfred

II. Short Answer

1 Explain Henry's role in the story.

2. Compare and contrast Alfred and James.

Contender Advanced Short Answer Unit Test Page 2

3. Explain the influences of these people on Alfred: Henry, Donatelli, Epstein, Spoon, Aunt Pearl, James.

4. Time is a factor in the story. Explain the importance of "time" in the story.

5. Several times in the story, people and situations aren't what they appear to be. Give at least two different examples from the text.

6. Why is the fact that Henry bought Alfred's robe symbolically important?

7. What activities in the book are presented as being positive things? What things are negative?

Contender Advanced Short Answer Unit Test Page 3

III. Quotations - Explain the importance or significance of each of the following quotations.

1. People will try to drag you down. (Donatelli, Ch.3)

2. Everybody is somebody. (Donatelli, Ch.3)

3. You have to start by wanting to be a contender, the man coming up, the man who knows there's a good chance he'll never get to the top, the man who's willing to sweat and bleed to get up as high as his legs and his brains and his heart will take him. (Donatelli, Ch.3)

4. It's the climbing that makes the man. Getting to the top is an extra reward. (Donatelli, Ch.3)

5. And nothing's promised you, nothing's ever promised you. (Donatelli, Ch.3)

6. Hang in there, Al, you're lookin' good. (Policeman, Ch.9)

7. Not like the old days when Alfred would follow James up to a corner of the balcony and root for the monster and cheer the Indians and afterward change the ending of the picture if they didn't like how it came out. (Alfred, Ch. 10)

8. Get up, go to work, go home and sleep so you can work some more and pay for your fun on the weekend. And then it's Monday again. Days move so slow. (Alfred, Ch.12)

9. You should have your own mind, do what you want. (Epstein, Ch.13)

Contender Advanced Short Answer Unit Test page 4

IV. Vocabulary

Listen to the vocabulary words and write them down. After you have written down all the words, write a paragraph using all of the vocabulary words. The paragraph must in some way relate to *The Contender*.

MULTIPLE CHOICE UNIT TEST 1 - *The Contender*

I. Matching/Identify

___ 1. Jelly Belly   A. Handicapped trainer and friend to Alfred

___ 2. Alfred   B. Manager

___ 3. James   C. "Look for opportunities for the future"

___ 4. Spoon   D. Ex-fighter, Alfred's boss at work

___ 5. Henry   E. The "contender"

___ 6. Bud   F. Bully, gang-leader

___ 7. Aunt Pearl   G. Tried to recruit Alfred to nationalist rally

___ 8. Uncle Wilson   H. Raised Alfred

___ 9. Major   I. Best friend of Alfred

___ 10. Lynn   J. Lacked self-discipline with food

___ 11. Donatelli   K. Knocked out James

___ 12. Epstein   L. The cut-man; assistant manager

                            M. Ex-fighter, teacher

Contender Multiple Choice Unit Test 1 Page 2

II. Multiple Choice

1. How is Alfred different from the gang at the clubroom?
    A. He carries a knife instead of a gun.
    B. He is the only one who can read.
    C. He is the only one who wants to admit girls to the club.
    D. He works and goes to church and tries to stay out of trouble.

2. What did Major, Hollis, and Sonny do to Alfred after their trip to Epstein's?
    A. They beat him up.
    B. They turned him upside down and shook all of the money out of his pockets.
    C. They kicked him out of the club.
    D. They congratulated him and told him what a great guy he was.

3. Why did Alfred first go to Donatelli's Gym?
    A. He thought he might be able to get a better paying job there.
    B. He hoped to get free tickets to some fights. He thought he could impress James if he took him to a fight.
    C. He did it on a dare from Henry.
    D. He was tired of being afraid of stronger gang members, and he wanted to be somebody, a champion.

4. Describe the relationship between James and Alfred.
    A. They were second cousins and enjoyed each other's company.
    B. They had met within the last year and were just getting to know each other, although they got along right away.
    C. They didn't really like each other, but they hung out together because they had mutual friends.
    D. They were best friends as kids. They were slowly growing apart as young adults.

5. Why did Alfred go back to the clubroom?
    A. He wanted to see James, and he was frustrated with what he felt was a lack of progress in his boxing career.
    B. Major had told him that a girl he (Alfred) liked would be there. Alfred went to impress her with his muscles and fancy footwork.
    C. He went with the intention of beating up Major, but changed his mind.
    D. He wanted to try and convince the others to give up their non-productive ways and join the gym.

Contender Multiple Choice Unit Test 1 Page 3

6. What did Alfred discover about his Aunt Pearl?
    A. She loved him as much as she loved her own children.
    B. She was even more stubborn than he had realized.
    C. She had once dreamed of being a singer, but never had the chance to reach for her dream.
    D. Her husband had been a boxer, and had died of a blow to the head. That was why she disliked boxing.

7. Why did Alfred feel sick after his second fight?
    A. He had eaten his dinner too quickly, and too close to fight time. It made him feel sluggish and sick.
    B. He knocked out Griffin. The thought that he could have really hurt or killed his opponent made him sick.
    C. Dr. Corey had given him an injection of steroids, and he had an adverse reaction to them.
    D. He couldn't block out the jeers and taunts from the crowd, and hearing their insults demoralized him.

8. Who was the shuddering old man who crouched along side Alfred's stairs?
    A. It was James, looking for drug money.
    B. It was one of Donatelli's former pupils, warning Alfred that he could end up on the street, too.
    C. It was no one special, just a homeless drunk. The encounter made Alfred realize what a good life he had.
    D. It was Henry's grandfather. He was ill, and sometimes wandered the streets. Alfred took him back home.

9. What did Alfred do for James?
    A. He took him home, cleaned him up, and fed him.
    B. He turned him over to the police for his own good.
    C. He took him to a hospital and said he would help him get straight.
    D. He gave James enough money to last for a few weeks.

Contender Multiple Choice Unit Test 1 Page 4

III. Quotations - Identify the speaker of each quote:

A=Alfred   B=Epstein   C=Donatelli   D=Pearl   E=Wilson   F=Bud
G=James   H=Lynn   I=Major   J=Henry   K=Policeman

1. The, uh, old stone fence off Lenox, Aunt Pearl. I was walking on it, and . . . a . . . a big dog jumped up. Knocked me off."

2. Stay in bed, man, curl up like a baby, close your eyes, make the world go away."

3. People will try to drag you down.

4. Everybody is somebody.

5. It's the climbing that makes the man. Getting to the top is an extra reward.

6. You're a good boy, Alfred, we all think you're a good boy. I told the police not to bother you. But sometimes it's hard to . . . well, we trust you, but for your own sake there's no point tempting fate. You understand.

7. Don't nobody tell the boss about this. Everybody gets a second chance around here.

8. Hang in there, Al, you're lookin' good.

9. He found a feature up on 125th Street, and went in. He had seen all the pictures on television already. So what. See them again, see them a thousand times, the new ones are the same as the old ones anyway.

10. Get up, go to work, go home and sleep so you can work some more and pay for your fun on the weekend. And then it's Monday again. Days move so slow.

11. You should have your own mind, do what you want.

12. Before the summer you didn't know about boxing neither.

13. At least you've done something.

14. Always got to be planning for the future, thinking ahead. Wake up one morning and you find the world passed you by.

15. Times are really changing.

IV. Composition

Explain how the events in Alfred's life changed him from the beginning of the story to the end.

Contender Multiple Choice Unit Test 1 Page 6

V. Vocabulary - Match the correct definitions to the words.

_____ 1. IMPATIENTLY   A. In a refined manner; classically beautifully

_____ 2. EMBLEM   B. Hallway

_____ 3. SULLEN   C. With reserve; showing decorum; with dignity

_____ 4. ELEGANTLY   D. A rundown, low-rent apartment building

_____ 5. CHAUFFEUR   E. Restlessly; anxiously

_____ 6. TENEMENT   F. Insignia; symbolic badge or design

_____ 7. SHRUGGED   G. Gloomy

_____ 8. PARALYZING   H. In a trance

_____ 9. PUMMELING   I. Passed; expired

_____ 10. AMATEUR   J. Hitting with an open hand

_____ 11. HYPNOTIZED   K. Turned towards one side

_____ 12. CUFFING   L. Continuing without interruption

_____ 13. LURCHED   M. Beating with fists

_____ 14. LAPSED   N. Making unable to move or act

_____ 15. DIGNIFIED   O. Moved shoulders up and down as a gesture of doubt or indifference

_____ 16. VEERED   P. Dependent on a habit-forming substance

_____ 17. CORRIDOR   Q. One employed to drive an automobile

_____ 18. ADDICT   R. Mixed

_____ 19. MINGLED   S. Rolled or pitched suddenly or erratically

_____ 20. PERPETUAL   T. A person who does an activity as a hobby instead of for pay

MULTIPLE CHOICE UNIT TEST 2 - *The Contender*

I. Matching/Identify

___ 1. Jelly Belly   A. Manager

___ 2. Alfred   B. Best friend of Alfred

___ 3. James   C. Tried to recruit Alfred to nationalist rally

___ 4. Spoon   D. The "contender"

___ 5. Henry   E. Bully, gang-leader

___ 6. Bud   F. Ex-fighter, Alfred's boss at work

___ 7. Aunt Pearl   G. Raised Alfred

___ 8. Uncle Wilson   H. "Look for opportunities for the future"

___ 9. Major   I. Lacked self-discipline with food

___ 10. Lynn   J. Ex-fighter, teacher

___ 11. Donatelli   K. The cut-man; assistant manager

___ 12. Epstein   L. Knocked out James

                               M. Handicapped trainer and friend to Alfred

II. Multiple Choice

1. How is Alfred different from the gang at the clubroom?
     A. He carries a knife instead of a gun.
     B. He works and goes to church and tries to stay out of trouble.
     C. He is the only one who wants to admit girls to the club.
     D. He is the only one who can read.

Contender Multiple Choice Unit Test 2 Page 2

2. What did Major, Hollis, and Sonny do to Alfred after their trip to Epstein's?
    A. They kicked him out of the club.
    B. They turned him upside down and shook all of the money out of his pockets.
    C. They beat him up.
    D. They congratulated him and told him what a great guy he was.

3. Why did Alfred first go to Donatelli's Gym?
    A. He was tired of being afraid of stronger gang members, and he wanted to be somebody, a champion.
    B. He hoped to get free tickets to some fights. He thought he could impress James if he took him to a fight.
    C. He did it on a dare from Henry.
    D. He thought he might be able to get a better paying job there.

4. Describe the relationship between James and Alfred.
    A. They were second cousins and enjoyed each other's company.
    B. They had met within the last year and were just getting to know each other, although they got along right away.
    C. They were best friends as kids. They were slowly growing apart as young adults.
    D. They didn't really like each other, but they hung out together because they had mutual friends.

5. Why did Alfred go back to the clubroom?
    A. He wanted to try and convince the others to give up their non-productive ways and join the gym.
    B. Major had told him that a girl he (Alfred) liked would be there. Alfred went to impress her with his muscles and fancy footwork.
    C. He went with the intention of beating up Major, but changed his mind.
    D. He wanted to see James, and he was frustrated with what he felt was a lack of progress in his boxing career.

6. What did Alfred discover about his Aunt Pearl?
    A. She loved him as much as she loved her own children.
    B. She had once dreamed of being a singer, but never had the chance to reach for her dream.
    C. She was even more stubborn than he had realized.
    D. Her husband had been a boxer, and had died of a blow to the head. That was why she disliked boxing.

Contender Multiple Choice Unit Test 2 Page 3

7. Why did Alfred feel sick after his second fight?
   A. He had eaten his dinner too quickly, and too close to fight time. It made him feel sluggish and sick.
   B. He couldn't block out the jeers and taunts from the crowd, and hearing their insults demoralized him.
   C. Dr. Corey had given him an injection of steroids, and he had an adverse reaction to them.
   D. He knocked out Griffin. The thought that he could have really hurt or killed his opponent made him sick.

8. Who was the shuddering old man who crouched along side Alfred's stairs?
   A. It was no one special, just a homeless drunk. The encounter made Alfred realize what a good life he had.
   B. It was one of Donatelli's former pupils, warning Alfred that he could end up on the street, too.
   C. It was James, looking for drug money.
   D. It was Henry's grandfather. He was ill, and sometimes wandered the streets. Alfred took him back home.

9. What did Alfred do for James?
   A. He took him to a hospital and said he would help him get straight.
   B. He turned him over to the police for his own good.
   C. He took him home, cleaned him up, and fed him.
   D. He gave James enough money to last for a few weeks.

Contender Multiple Choice Unit Test 2 Page 4

III. Quotations - Identify the speaker of each quote:

A=Pearl B=James C=Major D=Policeman E=Epstein F=Bud
G=Wilson H=Donatelli I=Lynn J=Henry K=Alfred

1. The, uh, old stone fence off Lenox, Aunt Pearl. I was walking on it, and . . . a . . . a big dog jumped up. Knocked me off."

2. Stay in bed, man, curl up like a baby, close your eyes, make the world go away."

3. People will try to drag you down.

4. Everybody is somebody.

5. It's the climbing that makes the man. Getting to the top is an extra reward.

6. You're a good boy, Alfred, we all think you're a good boy. I told the police not to bother you. But sometimes it's hard to . . . well, we trust you, but for your own sake there's no point tempting fate. You understand.

7. Don't nobody tell the boss about this. Everybody gets a second chance around here.

8. Hang in there, Al, you're lookin' good.

9. He found a feature up on 125th Street, and went in. He had seen all the pictures on television already. So what. See them again, see them a thousand times, the new ones are the same as the old ones anyway.

10. Get up, go to work, go home and sleep so you can work some more and pay for your fun on the weekend. And then it's Monday again. Days move so slow.

11. You should have your own mind, do what you want.

12. Before the summer you didn't know about boxing neither.

13. At least you've done something.

14. Always got to be planning for the future, thinking ahead. Wake up one morning and you find the world passed you by.

15. Times are really changing.

Contender Multiple Choice Unit Test 2 Page 5

IV. Composition

    What is the single most important event in Alfred's life during the time of the book, and what one person has the most influence on him during the same period? Use specific examples from the book to support your statements.

Contender Multiple Choice Unit Test 2 Page 6

V. Vocabulary - Match the correct definitions to the words.

____ 1. PERPETUAL   A. Gloomy

____ 2. CONCENTRATED   B. Moved shoulders up and down as a gesture of doubt or indifference

____ 3. SILHOUETTED   C. Indistinctly; unclearly

____ 4. SULLEN   D. Turned towards one side

____ 5. VEERED   E. That which goes before or prepares

____ 6. ENCASED   F. Passed; expired

____ 7. PURSUIT   G. A loud burst of noise

____ 8. LISTLESSNESS   H. Activity engaged in regularly; an endeavor

____ 9. HYPNOTIZED   I. Continuing without interruption

____ 10. FUNKY   J. Hum-drum; lifelessness; boredom

____ 11. ELEGANTLY   K. A rundown, low-rent apartment building

____ 12. LAPSED   L. Enclosed

____ 13. SHRUGGED   M. One employed to drive an automobile

____ 14. PRELIMINARY   N. In a trance

____ 15. TENEMENT   O. In a refined manner; classically beautifully

____ 16. CHAUFFEUR   P. Diligently thought about; focused

____ 17. ADDICT   Q. Earthy and uncomplicated; natural

____ 18. MINGLED   R. Dependent on a habit-forming substance

____ 19. PEAL   S. Mixed

____ 20. VAGUELY   T. Seen as a dark outline against a light background

ANSWER SHEET - *The Contender*
Multiple Choice Unit Tests

I. Matching	II. Multiple Choice	III. Quotes	IV. Vocabulary
1. ___	1. ___	1. ___	1. ___
2. ___	2. ___	2. ___	2. ___
3. ___	3. ___	3. ___	3. ___
4. ___	4. ___	4. ___	4. ___
5. ___	5. ___	5. ___	5. ___
6. ___	6. ___	6. ___	6. ___
7. ___	7. ___	7. ___	7. ___
8. ___	8. ___	8. ___	8. ___
9. ___	9. ___	9. ___	9. ___
10. ___		10. ___	10. ___
11. ___		11. ___	11. ___
12. ___		12. ___	12. ___
		13. ___	13. ___
		14. ___	14. ___
		15. ___	15. ___
			16. ___
			17. ___
			18. ___
			19. ___
			20. ___

ANSWER KEY MULTIPLE CHOICE UNIT TESTS – *The Contender*

Answers to Unit Test 1 are in the left column. Answers to Unit Test 2 are in the right column.

I. Matching	II. Multiple Choice	III. Quotes	IV. Vocabulary
1. J I	1. D B	1. A K	1. E I
2. E D	2. A C	2. A K	2. F P
3. I B	3. D A	3. C H	3. G T
4. M J	4. D C	4. C H	4. A A
5. A M	5. A D	5. C H	5. Q D
6. L K	6. C B	6. B E	6. D L
7. H G	7. B D	7. F F	7. O H
8. C H	8. A C	8. K D	8. N J
9. F E	9. C A	9. A K	9. M N
10. G C		10. A K	10. T Q
11. B A		11. B E	11. H O
12. D F		12. D A	12. J F
		13. H I	13. S B
		14. E G	14. I E
		15. E G	15. C K
			16. K M
			17. B R
			18. P S
			19. R G
			20. L C

UNIT RESOURCE MATERIALS

BULLETIN BOARD IDEAS - *The Contender*

1. Save one corner of the board for the best of students' *Contender* writing assignments.

2. Use the bulletin board suggestion from the introductory activity in Lesson One.

3. Take one of the word search puzzles from the extra activities section and with a marker copy it over in a large size on the bulletin board. Write the clue words to find to one side. Invite students prior to and after class to find the words and circle them on the bulletin board.

4. Do a bulletin board about careers in sports and sports-related fields: playing or managing, manufacturing or retailing sports equipment, running a gym or health club, sports medicine, etc.

5. Do a bulletin board with information about youth crisis hotlines.

6. Arrange the characters' names in cut-out letters on the board. Cut out pictures of people in magazines who look like each of the characters. Arrange the "good guys" on one side and the "bad guys" on the other with Alfred in the middle. Use yarn or string to represent the characters' pulling Alfred in different directions.

7. Write several of the most significant quotations from the book onto the board on brightly colored paper.

8. Make a bulletin board listing the vocabulary words for this unit. As you complete sections of the novel and discuss the vocabulary for each section, write the definitions on the bulletin board. (If your board is one students face frequently, it will help them learn the words.)

9. Do a bulletin board about boxers and boxing as a sport. Include some history of the sport, photos and biographies of famous boxers, etc.

10. Title the board BE A CONTENDER. Put the "don'ts" (things that would keep one from being a contender -- drugs, alcohol, crime, gangs) on one side and put "dos" (things that will help one be a contender -- school, goals, athletics, hobbies, work) on the other.

11. Do an anti-drug bulletin board. See your guidance office for info to post.

EXTRA ACTIVITIES - *The Contender*

One of the difficulties in teaching a novel is that all students don't read at the same speed. One student who likes to read may take the book home and finish it in a day or two. Sometimes a few students finish the in-class assignments early. The problem, then, is finding suitable extra activities for students.

One thing you can do is to keep a little library in the classroom. For this unit on *The Contender*, you might check out from the school library other related books and articles about boxing, sports, people who have risen from the ghetto to become successful, careers related to sports, and "how to" books about setting goals and achieving them. Articles or books about the author, this book, and his other works would be interesting, too.

Other things you may keep on hand are puzzles. We have made some relating directly to *The Contender* for you. Feel free to duplicate them.

Some students may like to draw. You might devise a contest or allow some extra-credit grade for students who draw characters or scenes from *The Contender*. Note, too, that if the students do not want to keep their drawings you may pick up some extra bulletin board materials this way. If you have a contest and you supply the prize (a CD or something like that perhaps), you could, possibly, make the drawing itself a non-returnable entry fee.

The pages which follow contain games, puzzles and worksheets. The keys, when appropriate, immediately follow the puzzle or worksheet. There are two main groups of activities: one group for the unit; that is, generally relating to the *Contender* text, and another group of activities related strictly to the *Contender* vocabulary.

Directions for these games, puzzles and worksheets are self-explanatory. The object here is to provide you with extra materials you may use in any way you choose.

MORE ACTIVITIES - *The Contender*

1. Pick a chapter or scene with a great deal of dialogue and have the students act it out on a stage. (Perhaps you could assign various scenes to different groups of students so more than one scene could be acted and more students could participate.)

2. Get a professional athlete to come to your class to speak about how he/she achieved his/her goals.

3. Spend some time talking about opportunities that exist for minorities, programs that are intended to help people get out of the ghetto life if they want to do so.

4. Have students design a book cover (front and back and inside flaps) for *The Contender*.

5. Have students design a bulletin board (ready to be put up; not just sketched) for *The Contender*.

6. Hold a class about black history, black heritage. Examine the biographies of several black men and women who have overcome a disadvantaged background to become successful.

7. Have your class discuss how they can improve the quality of life in their neighborhoods just by working within their own communities and using the resources currently available to them.

8. Do a group writing assignment to write the plot for a sequel to *The Contender*.

WORD SEARCH - *The Contender*

All words in this list are associated with *The Contender*. The words are placed backwards, forward, diagonally, up and down. The included words are listed below the word search.

```
K B L W R D G Z Y G V N W W W Q W D S Y V N G S
K C R M P W E Z M D D W N Y G J B K L P T C G M
C Z V O V K Z R Y Y O R C T A Q L S X F O U H Y
J H F H O S P G F T I B X M C N I M N P R O R G
G Y S I C K J E L L Y P E A R L M I N D L Y N N
D R G L R C S L L M A S D M L P U Y U F O I G R
T M I A I D D E S A O M F O O G R B G M B W T T
Z R P F N P T V M J L W H R E S Y N H M A E N N
R S A E F A S A K I R A A E G P O M I O R J C L
K B I I N I D Y D D T E R L N S S L M O U T O R
T R N O N I N V T H F M X M L R C T T L K S J R
F K D V S I N K V E P D M I C T Y S E T V B E P
C G T O R Y N J P J E T W Y K O R P Z I W X Z V
W L N G B B F G V S R R W R F C N D M L N B B L
Q Z H D W H N M I S P N G B J M N T W M M M P B
R K S D Z W H M N X L P J F Y M M W E H Z X W P
Q W G V K L O V D S J B P X M W L T T N C J N V
V W D T L R N L K B J R W S K K X M F G D Z N X
N Z M Z P Q H J D P X L S V M C K T B Y V E D S
D B F K N C C B F Q L H V Q G P L K Y C Y L R N
```

ALARM	DRUGS	JELLY	PROMISED
ALFRED	EPSTEIN	JOSE	SICK
BROOKS	FEAR	LIPSYTE	SOMEBODY
BUD	FRIENDS	LYNN	SPOON
CLIMBING	GRIFFIN	MADISON	STORE
CLUBHOUSE	GYM	MAJOR	TIMES
CONTENDER	HENRY	MIND	TRAINING
DONATELLI	HOLLIS	PARK	WALL
DOWN	JAMES	PEARL	WILSON

KEY: WORD SEARCH - *The Contender*

All words in this list are associated with *The Contender*. The words are placed backwards, forward, diagonally, up and down. The included words are listed below the word search.

```
            B           D        Y                              S              S
              R           E        D              J                P        G
                O           R        O              A       S        O U
                  O           F  I  B  M  C  I                R O        G
            G  S  I  C  K  J  E  L  L  Y  P  E  A  R  L  M  I  N  D  L  Y  N  N
              R  L  R     S     L     A  S     M     L     U     U        O  I
            T  I  A  I  D     E     A  O        O  G     B     M  B        W
              R  P  F  N  P  T     M  J  L  W  H  R  E  S  Y  N  H  M  A  E  N
              A  E  F  A  S  A     I     A  A  E     P  O  M  I  O  R  J
              I  I  N  I  D  Y        T  E  R  L  N  S  S  L     O  U     O
              R     O  N  I  N     T     F     M  L  R  C  T  T        S     R
            F     D     S  I           E     D     I  C     Y  S  E              E
                     O        N              E     W           O           I
                  N              G        S                       N           N
                              I                                T
                           M                                E
                        O                                      N
                     R                                            D
                  P                                                  E
                                                                        R
```

ALARM	DRUGS	JELLY	PROMISED
ALFRED	EPSTEIN	JOSE	SICK
BROOKS	FEAR	LIPSYTE	SOMEBODY
BUD	FRIENDS	LYNN	SPOON
CLIMBING	GRIFFIN	MADISON	STORE
CLUBHOUSE	GYM	MAJOR	TIMES
CONTENDER	HENRY	MIND	TRAINING
DONATELLI	HOLLIS	PARK	WALL
DOWN	JAMES	PEARL	WILSON

CROSSWORD PUZZLE The Contender

Across
1. Alfred knocked him out in his 2nd fight
3. Alfred's last name
6. '____ are really changing'
8. 'People will try to drag you____'
10. ____Belly; lacked self-discipline with food
12. James was hooked on these
14. Alfred's aunt
15. How Alfred felt after his 2nd fight
17. Ex-fighter; teacher
18. Alfred knocked him down while sparring
21. Bully; gang leader
22. Handicapped trainer and friend to Alfred
23. 'Nothing's____you, nothing's ever ____ you'
25. The contender; he boxes and works
26. Practicing

Down
1. Place to work out and practice boxing
2. Relationship between Alfred and James
3. The 'cut man'; assistant manager
4. 'Everybody is ____'
5. Epstein's establishment
7. Ex-fighter; Alfred's boss
9. Alfred told his aunt a dog knocked him off a stone ____
11. Author
13. ____ Square Garden
16. The____
18. Alfred's best friend
19. 'A man must have some____'
20. Tried to recruit Alfred
23. Place Alfred liked to run
24. 'You should have your own____, do what you want'

CROSSWORD ANSWER KEY The Contender

Across
1. Alfred knocked him out in his 2nd fight
3. Alfred's last name
6. '____ are really changing'
8. 'People will try to drag you____'
10. ____Belly; lacked self-discipline with food
12. James was hooked on these
14. Alfred's aunt
15. How Alfred felt after his 2nd fight
17. Ex-fighter; teacher
18. Alfred knocked him down while sparring
21. Bully; gang leader
22. Handicapped trainer and friend to Alfred
23. 'Nothing's____you, nothing's ever ____ you'
25. The contender; he boxes and works
26. Practicing

Down
1. Place to work out and practice boxing
2. Relationship between Alfred and James
3. The 'cut man'; assistant manager
4. 'Everybody is ____'
5. Epstein's establishment
7. Ex-fighter; Alfred's boss
9. Alfred told his aunt a dog knocked him off a stone ____
11. Author
13. ____ Square Garden
16. The____
18. Alfred's best friend
19. 'A man must have some____'
20. Tried to recruit Alfred
23. Place Alfred liked to run
24. 'You should have your own____, do what you want'

MATCHING QUIZ/WORKSHEET 1 - *The Contender*

____ 1. MAJOR   A. Alfred knocked him down while sparring

____ 2. PROMISED   B. *The ----*

____ 3. MADISON   C. How Alfred felt after his 2nd fight

____ 4. STORE   D. Bully; gang leader

____ 5. HENRY   E. Epstein's establishment

____ 6. PEARL   F. Alfred's aunt

____ 7. CLIMBING   G. Place to work out and practice boxing

____ 8. GYM   H. Place Alfred liked to run

____ 9. ALFRED   I. Alfred forgot to tell the gang about it

____ 10. JOSE   J. --- Square Garden

____ 11. BUD   K. Alfred's best friend

____ 12. CONTENDER   L. 'Nothing's --- you, nothing's ever --- you'

____ 13. PARK   M. The contender; he boxes and works

____ 14. ALARM   N. 'A man must have some ----'

____ 15. FEAR   O. Handicapped trainer and friend to Alfred

____ 16. SICK   P. 'It's the --- that makes the man'

____ 17. JAMES   Q. The 'cut man'; assistant manager

____ 18. DOWN   R. 'People will try to drag you ----'

____ 19. GRIFFIN   S. Alfred knocked him out in his 2nd fight

____ 20. LYNN   T. Tried to recruit Alfred

KEY: MATCHING QUIZ/WORKSHEET 1 - *The Contender*

__D__ 1. MAJOR   A. Alfred knocked him down while sparring

__L__ 2. PROMISED   B. *The* ----

__J__ 3. MADISON   C. How Alfred felt after his 2nd fight

__E__ 4. STORE   D. Bully; gang leader

__O__ 5. HENRY   E. Epstein's establishment

__F__ 6. PEARL   F. Alfred's aunt

__P__ 7. CLIMBING   G. Place to work out and practice boxing

__G__ 8. GYM   H. Place Alfred liked to run

__M__ 9. ALFRED   I. Alfred forgot to tell the gang about it

__A__ 10. JOSE   J. --- Square Garden

__Q__ 11. BUD   K. Alfred's best friend

__B__ 12. CONTENDER   L. 'Nothing's --- you, nothing's ever --- you'

__H__ 13. PARK   M. The contender; he boxes and works

__I__ 14. ALARM   N. 'A man must have some ----'

__N__ 15. FEAR   O. Handicapped trainer and friend to Alfred

__C__ 16. SICK   P. 'It's the --- that makes the man'

__K__ 17. JAMES   Q. The 'cut man'; assistant manager

__R__ 18. DOWN   R. 'People will try to drag you ----'

__S__ 19. GRIFFIN   S. Alfred knocked him out in his 2nd fight

__T__ 20. LYNN   T. Tried to recruit Alfred

MATCHING QUIZ/WORKSHEET 2 - *The Contender*

____ 1. JAMES   A. 'You should have your own ---, do what you want'

____ 2. CLIMBING   B. Ex-fighter; Alfred's boss

____ 3. LYNN   C. *The ----*

____ 4. WILSON   D. Alfred's aunt

____ 5. MIND   E. '--- are really changing'

____ 6. HENRY   F. How Alfred felt after his 2nd fight

____ 7. DRUGS   G. Alfred's last name

____ 8. HOLLIS   H. Alfred told his aunt a dog knocked him off of a stone ---

____ 9. TIMES   I. Handicapped trainer and friend to Alfred

____ 10. ALFRED   J. Alfred's best friend

____ 11. WALL   K. The contender; he boxes and works

____ 12. PARK   L. 'It's the --- that makes the man'

____ 13. CONTENDER   M. Relationship between Alfred and James

____ 14. BROOKS   N. He says to look for opportunities for the future

____ 15. EPSTEIN   O. 'Everybody is -----'

____ 16. FRIENDS   P. James was hooked on these

____ 17. SICK   Q. Place Alfred liked to run

____ 18. SOMEBODY   R. Tried to recruit Alfred

____ 19. DOWN   S. He, Major & Sonny beat up Alfred

____ 20. PEARL   T. 'People will try to drag you ----'

KEY: MATCHING QUIZ/WORKSHEET 2 - *The Contender*

__J__	1. JAMES	A. 'You should have your own ---, do what you want'
__L__	2. CLIMBING	B. Ex-fighter; Alfred's boss
__R__	3. LYNN	C. *The* ----
__N__	4. WILSON	D. Alfred's aunt
__A__	5. MIND	E. '--- are really changing'
__I__	6. HENRY	F. How Alfred felt after his 2nd fight
__P__	7. DRUGS	G. Alfred's last name
__S__	8. HOLLIS	H. Alfred told his aunt a dog knocked him off of a stone ---
__E__	9. TIMES	I. Handicapped trainer and friend to Alfred
__K__	10. ALFRED	J. Alfred's best friend
__H__	11. WALL	K. The contender; he boxes and works
__Q__	12. PARK	L. 'It's the --- that makes the man'
__C__	13. CONTENDER	M. Relationship between Alfred and James
__G__	14. BROOKS	N. He says to look for opportunities for the future
__B__	15. EPSTEIN	O. 'Everybody is -----'
__M__	16. FRIENDS	P. James was hooked on these
__F__	17. SICK	Q. Place Alfred liked to run
__O__	18. SOMEBODY	R. Tried to recruit Alfred
__T__	19. DOWN	S. He, Major & Sonny beat up Alfred
__D__	20. PEARL	T. 'People will try to drag you ----'

JUGGLE LETTER REVIEW GAME CLUE SHEET - *Contender*

SCRAMBLED	WORD	CLUE
MARLA	ALARM	Alfred forgot to tell the gang about it
LADRFE	ALFRED	The contender; he boxes and works
SOOBKR	BROOKS	Alfred's last name
DUB	BUD	The 'cut man'; assistant manager
MICNIGLB	CLIMBING	'It's the --- that makes the man'
LBSOUEHUC	CLUBHOUSE	Place where the gang meets
NEENDOTRC	CONTENDER	*The* ----
TONILELAD	DONATELLI	Boxing manager
WOND	DOWN	'People will try to drag you ----'
GRUDS	DRUGS	James was hooked on these
NEEPTIS	EPSTEIN	Ex-fighter; Alfred's boss
EARF	FEAR	'A man must have some ----'
RESFIND	FRIENDS	Relationship between Alfred and James
FINIRGF	GRIFFIN	Alfred knocked him out in his 2nd fight
MYG	GYM	Place to work out and practice boxing
HRYEN	HENRY	Handicapped trainer and friend to Alfred
LOHLSI	HOLLIS	He, Major & Sonny beat up Alfred
MEJAS	JAMES	Alfred's best friend
YLJEL	JELLY	--- Belly; lacked self-discipline with food
EOSJ	JOSE	Alfred knocked him down while sparring
TYSLPIE	LIPSYTE	Author
NYNL	LYNN	Tried to recruit Alfred
SAMDONI	MADISON	--- Square Garden
JAMOR	MAJOR	Bully; gang leader
DMNI	MIND	'You should have your own ---, do what you want'
RAPK	PARK	Place Alfred liked to run
LAPRE	PEARL	Alfred's aunt
RIDOPSEM	PROMISED	'Nothing's --- you, nothing's ever --- you'
KICS	SICK	How Alfred felt after his 2nd fight
ESDMOOYB	SOMEBODY	'Everybody is -----'
ONOPS	SPOON	Ex-fighter; teacher
EROTS	STORE	Epstein's establishment
METSI	TIMES	'--- are really changing'
NANTRIGI	TRAINING	Practicing
LAWL	WALL	Alfred told his aunt a dog knocked him off of a stone ---
WOLISN	WILSON	He says to look for opportunities for the future

VOCABULARY RESOURCE MATERIALS

VOCABULARY WORD SEARCH - *Contender*

All words in this list are associated with *The Contender* with an emphasis on the vocabulary words chosen for study in the text. The words are placed backwards, forward, diagonally, up and down. The included words are listed below.

```
I M P A T I E N T L Y Y L I S T L E S S N E S S
F Z F N K N D V D Z R L T J X H M S G P Q N B K
L G H B G C G G X A L W T Y Y C T N Y P G R G P
Y P U M M E L I N G H Y P N O T I Z E D R P W F
S F Y K V C W I F V R Z G K A F S H H U Y V X N
R Q Q J D T M S B G D B Y H F G L C E F Q K D B
H M J K Z I L K C X N K X U C H E T D X F E L D
V K F L L X R A B J S I C K Q O A L D R I H M G
B H X E Y C V N U L T K Z H J M R L E F Y P F T
F X R V Z V H H D T A B F Y A Q G R I B S Q V M
R P H V W M B H M Q E P N R L Y P N I F Y W D K
F S C D A X H P N Z C P S K J A G B V D U F L S
V K L L M U L E G J V T R E P I R T V P O N H D
N H L T S I L H O U E T T E D E S A C N E R K D
C L C M H L G T Q N I R A E P E G E P I U N E Y
Y C R M U Q Z L E U D L R C H U H H R G D L N F
Q N F S B T D M S D P E R G E J Z C G E G D Q V
E M B L E M E R P Q E W V L C V V E R N N P A Z
Y J C R Y N U D C V T K Y B R R D K I U Q E S S
M F J T T P C H A U F F E U R G S M R K L M Z G
```

ADDICT	ENCASED	MUTED	SHRUGGED
AMATEUR	FUNKY	PARALYZING	SILHOUETTED
CHAUFFEUR	HYPNOTIZED	PEAL	SULLEN
CORRIDOR	IMPATIENTLY	PERPETUAL	TENEMENT
CUFFING	LAPSED	PRELIMINARY	VAGUELY
DIGNIFIED	LISTLESSNESS	PUMMELING	VAULTED
ELEGANTLY	LURCHED	PURSUIT	VEERED
EMBLEM	MINGLED	SERENE	

KEY: VOCABULARY WORD SEARCH - *Contender*

All words in this list are associated with *The Contender* with an emphasis on the vocabulary words chosen for study in the text. The words are placed backwards, forward, diagonally, up and down. The included words are listed below.

```
I M P A T I E N T L Y Y L I S T L E S S N E S S
                  R L             G
            A     T         N
P U M M E L I N G H Y P N O T I Z E D R
          I           A F         U
        M   G         F G     E       D
      I L     N   U C   E T       E
    L       A       I C   O A L     I
  E           U L     Z   M R   E F
R               T A     Y A   R I
P   V             E P     L   N I F
      A       N     P S     A G   D U       S
        U   E       T R E P I R T V   O N H
        S I L H O U E T T E D E S A C N E R K D
      M   L   T   N I   A E P E G E P I U   E Y
          U       E U   L R     U H   R G D L
        S   T   M S D   E     E     C G E G D
  E M B L E M E R     E     L       E R N N   A
          N U D   V       Y       D   I U   E
        T P C H A U F F E U R       M     L
```

ADDICT	ENCASED	MUTED	SHRUGGED
AMATEUR	FUNKY	PARALYZING	SILHOUETTED
CHAUFFEUR	HYPNOTIZED	PEAL	SULLEN
CORRIDOR	IMPATIENTLY	PERPETUAL	TENEMENT
CUFFING	LAPSED	PRELIMINARY	VAGUELY
DIGNIFIED	LISTLESSNESS	PUMMELING	VAULTED
ELEGANTLY	LURCHED	PURSUIT	VEERED
EMBLEM	MINGLED	SERENE	

VOCABULARY CROSSWORD - *Contender*

VOCABULARY CROSSWORD CLUES - *The Contender*

ACROSS

4. A loud burst of noise
5. One employed to drive an automobile
11. Earthy and uncomplicated; natural
12. Gloomy
13. Dependent on a habit-forming substance
15. Abbreviation for avenue
17. Alfred said one knocked him off a stone wall
18. Alfred got a cut over his ---
19. Calm; unruffled
20. Muffled; sound made soft by distance or interference
21. Tried to recruit Alfred
22. Mr. Epstein gave Alfred the afternoon ---; without work
23. 'You should have your own ---, do what you want'
25. A short sleep time
26. Alfred told his aunt a dog knocked him off of a stone ---
28. Alfred --- to the gym to practice
29. Place to work out and practice boxing
30. Turned towards one side
31. Be victorious
32. Present plural of 'to be'
33. 'People will try to drag you ----'
35. 'A man must have some ----'
37. Bully; gang leader
39. Insignia; symbolic badge or design
41. --- Belly; lacked self-discipline with food
42. Alfred's aunt
43. James was hooked on these
45. Alfred knocked him down while sparring
46. Trousers made of a heavy cotton fabric, usually blue
47. The 'cut man'; assistant manager
48. Muscles --- after a good workout
49. Ex-fighter; teacher

DOWN

1. Passed; expired
2. Hitting with an open hand
3. Handicapped trainer and friend to Alfred
4. Making unable to move or act
5. Diligently thought about; focused
6. A person who does an activity as a hobby instead of for pay
7. Enclosed
8. In a trance
9. Hallway
10. In a refined manner; classically beautifully
14. With reserve; showing decorum; with dignity
16. That which goes before or prepares
20. Mixed
21. Author
24. Boxing manager
27. Rolled or pitched suddenly or erratically
34. He says to look for opportunities for the future
35. Relationship between Alfred and James
36. Alfred forgot to tell the gang about it
38. The contender; he boxes and works
40. Alfred's last name
41. Alfred's best friend
44. How Alfred felt after his 2nd fight

VOCABULARY CROSSWORD ANSWER KEY - *Contender*

VOCABULARY WORKSHEET 1 - *Contender*

____ 1. In a trance
    A. Funky   B. Lurched   C. Hypnotized   D. Pummeling

____ 2. Jumped
    A. Muted   B. Vaulted   C. Lurched   D. Encased

____ 3. Dependent on a habit-forming substance
    A. Corridor   B. Pursuit   C. Funky   D. Addict

____ 4. Activity engaged in regularly; an endeavor
    A. Silhouetted   B. Funky   C. Pursuit   D. Perpetual

____ 5. Making unable to move or act
    A. Tenement   B. Pummeling   C. Paralyzing   D. Encased

____ 6. Diligently thought about; focused
    A. Peal   B. Emblem   C. Concentrated   D. Muted

____ 7. Mixed
    A. Emblem   B. Concentrated   C. Mingled   D. Impatiently

____ 8. Gloomy
    A. Addict   B. Funky   C. Sullen   D. Paralyzing

____ 9. Indistinctly; unclearly
    A. Hypnotized   B. Elegantly   C. Impatiently   D. Vaguely

____ 10. Calm; unruffled
    A. Serene   B. Vaulted   C. Chauffeur   D. Emblem

____ 11. Earthy and uncomplicated; natural
    A. Dignified   B. Muted   C. Funky   D. Listlessness

____ 12. A rundown, low-rent apartment building
    A. Dignified   B. Tenement   C. Impatiently   D. Sullen

____ 13. Insignia; symbolic badge or design
    A. Lapsed   B. Serene   C. Emblem   D. Mingled

____ 14. A person who does an activity as a hobby instead of for pay
    A. Amateur   B. Chauffeur   C. Vaulted   D. Dignified

____ 15. Continuing without interruption
    A. Tenement   B. Muted   C. Impatiently   D. Perpetual

____ 16. A loud burst of noise
    A. Pummeling   B. Elegantly   C. Peal   D. Vaulted

____ 17. Turned towards one side
    A. Veered   B. Preliminary   C. Peal   D. Impatiently

____ 18. Muffled; sound made soft by distance or interference
    A. Cuffing   B. Lapsed   C. Muted   D. Sullen

____ 19. In a refined manner; classically beautifully
    A. Dignified   B. Shrugged   C. Perpetual   D. Elegantly

____ 20. Rolled or pitched suddenly or erratically
    A. Hypnotized   B. Vaulted   C. Lurched   D. Dignified

KEY: VOCABULARY WORKSHEET 1 - *Contender*

__C__ 1. In a trance
    A. Funky   B. Lurched   C. Hypnotized   D. Pummeling

__B__ 2. Jumped
    A. Muted   B. Vaulted   C. Lurched   D. Encased

__D__ 3. Dependent on a habit-forming substance
    A. Corridor   B. Pursuit   C. Funky   D. Addict

__C__ 4. Activity engaged in regularly; an endeavor
    A. Silhouetted   B. Funky   C. Pursuit   D. Perpetual

__C__ 5. Making unable to move or act
    A. Tenement   B. Pummeling   C. Paralyzing   D. Encased

__C__ 6. Diligently thought about; focused
    A. Peal   B. Emblem   C. Concentrated   D. Muted

__C__ 7. Mixed
    A. Emblem   B. Concentrated   C. Mingled   D. Impatiently

__C__ 8. Gloomy
    A. Addict   B. Funky   C. Sullen   D. Paralyzing

__D__ 9. Indistinctly; unclearly
    A. Hypnotized   B. Elegantly   C. Impatiently   D. Vaguely

__A__ 10. Calm; unruffled
    A. Serene   B. Vaulted   C. Chauffeur   D. Emblem

__C__ 11. Earthy and uncomplicated; natural
    A. Dignified   B. Muted   C. Funky   D. Listlessness

__B__ 12. A rundown, low-rent apartment building
    A. Dignified   B. Tenement   C. Impatiently   D. Sullen

__C__ 13. Insignia; symbolic badge or design
    A. Lapsed   B. Serene   C. Emblem   D. Mingled

__A__ 14. A person who does an activity as a hobby instead of for pay
    A. Amateur   B. Chauffeur   C. Vaulted   D. Dignified

__D__ 15. Continuing without interruption
    A. Tenement   B. Muted   C. Impatiently   D. Perpetual

__C__ 16. A loud burst of noise
    A. Pummeling   B. Elegantly   C. Peal   D. Vaulted

__A__ 17. Turned towards one side
    A. Veered   B. Preliminary   C. Peal   D. Impatiently

__C__ 18. Muffled; sound made soft by distance or interference
    A. Cuffing   B. Lapsed   C. Muted   D. Sullen

__D__ 19. In a refined manner; classically beautifully
    A. Dignified   B. Shrugged   C. Perpetual   D. Elegantly

__C__ 20. Rolled or pitched suddenly or erratically
    A. Hypnotized   B. Vaulted   C. Lurched   D. Dignified

VOCABULARY WORKSHEET 2 - *Contender*

____ 1. LISTLESSNESS   A. Seen as a dark outline against a light background

____ 2. ELEGANTLY   B. Mixed

____ 3. LAPSED   C. Dependent on a habit-forming substance

____ 4. PEAL   D. Hallway

____ 5. IMPATIENTLY   E. A loud burst of noise

____ 6. ADDICT   F. Restlessly; anxiously

____ 7. LURCHED   G. Hum-drum; lifelessness; boredom

____ 8. MINGLED   H. Continuing without interruption

____ 9. PUMMELING   I. Enclosed

____ 10. ENCASED   J. Earthy and uncomplicated; natural

____ 11. CONCENTRATED   K. Diligently thought about; focused

____ 12. AMATEUR   L. In a refined manner; classically beautifully

____ 13. PERPETUAL   M. Hitting with an open hand

____ 14. VEERED   N. A person who does an activity as a hobby instead of for pay

____ 15. CUFFING   O. Turned towards one side

____ 16. FUNKY   P. Rolled or pitched suddenly or erratically

____ 17. CORRIDOR   Q. Beating with fists

____ 18. SULLEN   R. Gloomy

____ 19. VAGUELY   S. Passed; expired

____ 20. SILHOUETTED   T. Indistinctly; unclearly

KEY: VOCABULARY WORKSHEET 2 - *Contender*

_G_	1. LISTLESSNESS	A. Seen as a dark outline against a light background
_L_	2. ELEGANTLY	B. Mixed
_S_	3. LAPSED	C. Dependent on a habit-forming substance
_E_	4. PEAL	D. Hallway
_F_	5. IMPATIENTLY	E. A loud burst of noise
_C_	6. ADDICT	F. Restlessly; anxiously
_P_	7. LURCHED	G. Hum-drum; lifelessness; boredom
_B_	8. MINGLED	H. Continuing without interruption
_Q_	9. PUMMELING	I. Enclosed
_I_	10. ENCASED	J. Earthy and uncomplicated; natural
_K_	11. CONCENTRATED	K. Diligently thought about; focused
_N_	12. AMATEUR	L. In a refined manner; classically beautifully
_H_	13. PERPETUAL	M. Hitting with an open hand
_O_	14. VEERED	N. A person who does an activity as a hobby instead of for pay
_M_	15. CUFFING	O. Turned towards one side
_J_	16. FUNKY	P. Rolled or pitched suddenly or erratically
_D_	17. CORRIDOR	Q. Beating with fists
_R_	18. SULLEN	R. Gloomy
_T_	19. VAGUELY	S. Passed; expired
_A_	20. SILHOUETTED	T. Indistinctly; unclearly

VOCABULARY JUGGLE LETTER REVIEW GAME CLUES - *Contender*

SCRAMBLED	WORD	CLUE
DADCIT	ADDICT	Dependent on a habit-forming substance
REAMUTA	AMATEUR	A person who does an activity as a hobby instead of for pay
REUHUFCAF	CHAUFFEUR	One employed to drive an automobile
NETDEROCCTAN	CONCENTRATED	Diligently thought about; focused
RIROORDC	CORRIDOR	Hallway
FINCFUG	CUFFING	Hitting with an open hand
DINDEIFIG	DIGNIFIED	With reserve; showing decorum; with dignity
YANEGLETL	ELEGANTLY	In a refined manner; classically beautifully
MEMBEL	EMBLEM	Insignia; symbolic badge or design
CADSEEN	ENCASED	Enclosed
YUNFK	FUNKY	Earthy and uncomplicated; natural
OIZDPHNEYT	HYPNOTIZED	In a trance
PENTATMIYIL	IMPATIENTLY	Restlessly; anxiously
DAPSEL	LAPSED	Passed; expired
SSSSEELLISTN	LISTLESSNESS	Hum-drum; lifelessness; boredom
HURDCEL	LURCHED	Rolled or pitched suddenly or erratically
GEMNILD	MINGLED	Mixed
UDTEM	MUTED	Muffled; sound made soft by distance or interference
NARPZYLAGI	PARALYZING	Making unable to move or act
LEAP	PEAL	A loud burst of noise
TERPLAUPE	PERPETUAL	Continuing without interruption
RIMPERYNIAL	PRELIMINARY	That which goes before or prepares
PUGMELMIN	PUMMELING	Beating with fists
PUSTIRU	PURSUIT	Activity engaged in regularly; an endeavor
SEENER	SERENE	Calm; unruffled
GHRUDEGS	SHRUGGED	Moved shoulders up and down as a gesture of doubt or indifference
LOHTEEDTUIS	SILHOUETTED	Seen as a dark outline against a light background
LULNES	SULLEN	Gloomy
NEETNETM	TENEMENT	A rundown, low-rent apartment building
VULGEYA	VAGUELY	Indistinctly; unclearly
DULVATE	VAULTED	Jumped
DREVEE	VEERED	Turned towards one side

www.ingramcontent.com/pod-product-compliance
Lightning Source LLC
Chambersburg PA
CBHW051417070526
44584CB00023B/3462